THE DON'T SWEAT GUIDE
FOR GRADUATES

Other books by the editors of Don't Sweat Press

The Don't Sweat Affirmations

The Don't Sweat Guide for Couples

The Don't Sweat Guide for Grandparents

The Don't Sweat Guide for Parents

The Don't Sweat Guide for Moms

The Don't Sweat Guide for Weddings

THE DON'T SWEAT GUIDE
FOR GRADUATES

Facing New Challenges
with Confidence

By the Editors of Don't Sweat Press
Foreword by Richard Carlson, Ph.D.,
author of the bestselling *Don't Sweat the Small Stuff*

New York

ISBN 0-7868-8725-7

FIRST EDITION

10 9 8 7 6 5 4 3 2 1

Contents

Foreword

Congratulations! You've done it. You've completed a process that you worked hard to achieve.

To me, there has always been something magical about graduating — whether it was high school, trade school, college, or whatever it might be. I consider these types of experiences to be a major cause for celebration! Much more than simply a sense of relief, there's a deep feeling of satisfaction and pride; a knowing that I set out to do something and it's done. A process is complete.

I love attending graduations, as well. Whether it's for one of my own kids, a family member, a friend, colleague, or a child of a friend, I enjoy seeing the pride of success in someone else's eyes. It's a look like no other because, very simply, graduating is unlike anything else. Instead of striving, rushing, studying for exams, and working to meet deadlines (which seems to be what were usually doing), we finally get a chance to simply enjoy the end result. And what's more, no one expects us to do anything else except enjoy it!

Graduation is a fork in the road. It's the proud and successful ending of one chapter of your life, and simultaneously, the beginning of another. It's a great time to reflect on your achievement. It might even be a great time to take a little time for yourself.

It is also, however, a time to look forward; a chance to reflect on the next phase of your life. In a very real sort of way, it's a new beginning. With a clear slate, a clear mind, and a heightened and renewed sense of energy, you have the opportunity to put new seeds into motion.

The editors of Don't Sweat Press have done a beautiful job in adding to the celebration of graduation. They have written this book in a way that enhances the spirit and joy of graduation, but that also encourages deep reflection. The strategies guide you to greater perspective and gratitude.

They also help with one more thing. Although our thinking is a tremendous gift, there are times when most of us use that gift against ourselves. In other words, we think too much, worry unnecessarily, blow things out of proportion, and get too stressed out! In a very gentle way, this book addresses these issues so that you will end up with the least amount of stress — and the most possible enjoyment.

As you complete one phase of your life and move on to another, I hope you take time out to congratulate yourself. I also hope this book enhances your perspective and gives you pause to reflect, as it has for me. Again, I send you my most sincere congratulations!

Richard Carlson

THE DON'T SWEAT GUIDE
FOR GRADUATES

1.

Take Time to Enjoy
Your Accomplishments

Graduating from college is an amazing feat. You've spent approximately four years of your life working toward a degree, building skills you'll need in the "real" world. Admittedly, you might not have spent all of your time at the library or with your head buried in a book. But ultimately, you did it! You worked hard to reach a goal, to cross the finish line, to earn that degree. It doesn't matter how many detours you may have taken along the way. You did it!

Your family is proud, and you should feel proud, too. Take time to enjoy your accomplishment. Graduating from college is a tremendous achievement. It doesn't matter if you changed your major a million times or if you missed a few exams because of spring break. The bottom line is that you did it! You deserve the praises others heap on you. Bask in their compliments, and savor the moment.

Then—when all the hoopla has died down, when the graduation dinners are over and the handshaking has stopped—take a moment to reflect. Recall how you felt during your first year, what your expectations might have been, or any fears or anxieties you had. Compare yourself as you were then with who you have become. Only four years may have passed, but so much has happened. Write down those experiences that mean the most to you. They can be academic experiences that made an impact on your class and career choices, or social experiences that helped you discover new things about yourself.

The things that you have written are what college was really all about. It was more than just signing up for classes, studying, and getting passing grades. College was a whole-life experience. The people you met and the things you did shaped who you are now. They broadened your mind and expanded your horizons.

That's part of the accomplishment. Graduating college means more than just receiving a degree. It means that you not only started something, but you finished it, too. You were able to juggle many responsibilities, both academic and social—and you survived!

Graduating from college can be a bittersweet moment, when one part of your life has ended and another is about to begin. Look back and appreciate what you have accomplished. Don't worry about what the next beginning will be. Simply enjoy the fact that you are now a college graduate. Congratulations!

2.

Give Yourself Some
Breathing Room

It's a given. As soon as the degree is in your hand, someone will ask the question that has probably been plaguing you since you donned your cap and gown: Now what?

It's one of the hardest questions that you will face—and one of the toughest questions to answer. The truth of the matter is that you have your entire life to work on your career. And once you step onto that career path, it's very hard to take yourself off it. You won't want to lose momentum, and you'll probably find yourself too engrossed in your career to want to, anyway.

Try not to feel pressured by the questions and expectations of others. Instead, take the time to really evaluate what you want to do. It might sound clichéd, but this is the perfect moment to stop and smell the flowers—or the coffee, as the case may be. There is absolutely no rule that says you have to start your career the moment that you graduate college.

Look at it this way: You're only in your twenties once. You probably don't have mortgage payments or a family to support. For the first time in four years, you don't have to answer to anyone but yourself. No teachers, no roommates, no schedules—your time is now your own. Take advantage of it! Do something that you always wanted to do, but never had time to do because of your schedule and school pressures. This doesn't mean starting your career. You might travel, write, or volunteer. Now is the perfect time to follow your heart.

It doesn't matter what you do, but if you're able, give yourself some breathing room between college and your career. It will help you to not only put college and a career in perspective, but to sort out any possible issues you might have with which way you want your career to go. These few weeks or months really won't make that much of a difference in the long run. Your career will still be there waiting for you when you're ready.

3.

Write Down Your Goals,
and Then Put the List Away

Like many people, you probably have goals now that you are out of college. In fact, parents and teachers will often drum into your head that if you don't have goals, you won't achieve what you want.

Okay, so sit down and write out your goals. List them all.

Then put the list away.

Admittedly, goals are great motivators. They should inspire you. They should make you want to seize the day, to work toward them, full-speed ahead.

However, rereading your list of goals on a daily basis can actually fill you with dread. After all, how stressful is it to be faced with things that you want to achieve when you're such a long way from achieving them? You may end up feeling discouraged and hopeless.

Writing down your goals is a wonderful exercise. It helps keep you in focus. It asks you to analyze what you really want out of life.

Your goals are actually part of your personality. But the only thing that makes your goals possible is you—not a list posted on your wall that reminds you of how far you still have to go.

Include on your list of goals everything you'd like to accomplish now that you are out of school. Write down your ideas, not only for jobs and careers, but for family and recreation. Having goals is more than just hoping to be CEO of a major company someday. Having goals is about life aspirations.

Remember, goals are great, but if they stress you out, they're defeating the purpose. You might choose one goal from your list that is easiest to attain right now. Then set the list aside and move on. Sometime down the road, you can take out your list and evaluate your progress, but for now, concentrate on a goal that you feel you have control over. The rest of your goals may just take a little longer.

4.

Rise to the Challenge of "What Now?"

So you've sidestepped the question and come up with vague answers to pacify friends and family. Now it's your turn to answer for yourself: "What now?"

Don't let the question bully you. Instead of hearing it as a negative—"Oh, no! What now?"—listen to the question as a challenge: "I finished college! What now? What else can I conquer?"

At this point, you don't have to look at this question as a life-altering proposition. Instead, think of something small you would like to do, and build on it. View your choice as the next step in a chain of challenges.

Of course, it's not always easy to rise to the occasion. The point is not to let the weight of your decision bog you down and stress you out. Yes, "What now?" can have lifelong implications. However, if you're confused or undecided, choose something that you can do

21

now, and do it the best that you can. Make something happen for yourself. Push yourself just a tiny bit to make that choice a reality. Pursue a job, take time out to follow a dream, or decide what you're *not* going to do.

When you finish school, people expect you to move on to "bigger and better" things. They're asking "What now?" out of curiosity and care, not to pressure you. The answer should be yours. It shouldn't be what you think others want you to do, or what you think they expect of you. It should be your challenge, your choice. View this next step as a series of challenges, and set out to conquer them all.

5.

Consider Graduate School

An option open to all college graduates is the possibility of attending graduate school. Several thoughts on this probably come to mind. There are a few things to consider when making this important decision. Thinking them all through will aid you in making choices.

First, ask yourself if you really enjoyed going to class. Did you enjoy learning and studying, researching and connecting with other students and your teachers? If the answer is yes—if going to graduate school is what you want to do and you can afford it—then do it. The heart of the matter is that it's what you want to do. This is your answer to "What now?" If it makes sense to you, then pursue this goal.

But someone may tell you that by the time you get out of school with your graduate degree, you'll still only be able to get an administrative assistant job. If you went right into the workforce, you could be two years ahead of yourself. This may be true, but who's to say? Who's to say that in graduate school you won't make a connection that will lead you to a higher position, or that academia won't be your career? Your career isn't going away. Does it matter if you are twenty-two or twenty-four when you start your entry-level job? In the end, it will all equal out.

Finally, if graduate school is where you see yourself, don't let others talk you out of it just because they feel you're "hiding" from "real" responsibilities. Graduate school *is* like a job, complete with goals, deadlines, and a payoff. Excelling in it is a job well done.

It's okay to consider graduate school as an option after college. Don't let others try to pressure you either way. Do what feels right for you, and it will be one less thing you have to worry about.

6.

Keep Your
Part-Time College Job

Graduating from college brings major changes. Your are no longer studying for exams and plowing through texts to write research papers. So excited are you to move on with your life that you're probably ready to leave behind everything associated with your college days, including your part-time job. In fact, some may even suggest that quitting your part-time job is the right thing to do. After all, looking for your "real" job is a full-time job, they explain.

However, there are several reasons to keep that part-time job. The most obvious is income. Unless you are independently wealthy or you don't mind asking parents, family, or friends for a loan, it is always less stressful to have your own money.

Another reason is flexibility. Most places of work that hire college students are used to managing flexible hours. The part-time job is ideal to keep while job-hunting. Working a combination of day and night shifts can help you budget your time. Suppose you had all the time in the world to put your resume together and go on interviews. With nothing on the horizon, with no job to fill your days, you might procrastinate. However, if tomorrow you have to work, you may use your free time more positively, realizing that other days are already booked.

A third reason to keep your part-time job is continuity. Once you leave college, so much is out of your control. Your part-time job can be something familiar to go back to. There is security in knowing what to expect and what is expected of you

When you consider the changes that you will make upon graduation, realize that it is beneficial to keep the part-time job that sustained you through your college days. It can only help you as you pursue future endeavors.

7.

Turn Your Achievements
into Positive Actions

It is often difficult to realize just what you are achieving while you are in the midst of it. What may seem like a ho-hum accomplishment to you might actually be pretty fantastic to someone else. Now is the time to evaluate your achievements and turn them into positive actions.

Your achievements say positive things about you. Finding a job is not always easy, especially if in a competitive field. Remembering your achievements will keep you positive. You will realize that you have already done so much. You can handle whatever comes next.

You have to be positive about yourself in order for someone to be positive about you. If you go into an interview or write your resume with the attitude, "I have nothing to offer anyone," chances are that a stranger will see this, as well. After all, if you don't think your accomplishments are special, why should a prospective boss think so?

Be excited about your achievements. They will help a potential employer figure out who you are and make you feel good about yourself. You'll make the person on the other side of the table sit up and take notice. Make your accomplishments work for you, and you'll reap the positive rewards.

8.

Live with
Family and Friends

One of the biggest stresses of the "real" world is having to pay bills. Along with all the other stresses in your life right now, worrying about rent, utilities, and the cable bill does not need to be among them.

Even though it seems like you should be out on your own now, accept that it is okay to live with friends or family. If the option is available, it will greatly reduce your financial worries, allowing you to concentrate on more important things.

Granted, living on your own is important, too. After all, that was one of the reasons you went to college. College is meant to provide you with enough education so that you can make it on your own. But you might not have that job yet, or you may only have a part-time job, so living on your own might just have to wait.

Having your own place gives a great sense of freedom. Yet how free will you feel when the electric bill comes? Or a repair needs to be made? Buying furniture is one more expense—and stress—you don't need right now.

Living with family or living with friends is a great alternative to living on your own, but each has its own ups and downs. When living with family, you might feel pressured to get a "real" job and put your college degree to work, when all you want to do is regroup. When living with friends, you might feel pressured to go out every night and party it up, when all you want to do is rest up for an interview. Living with family is often free; living with friends in a house or apartment usually requires that you foot your share of the bills.

Whichever scenario works best for you is fine. Just realize that because you're out of college doesn't mean you have to be completely on your own. Roommates—whether they are family or friends—can alleviate stress and be a great support, as well.

9.

Enjoy Being
in Your Twenties

You probably couldn't wait to grow up and be a teenager. Then you couldn't wait to get out of high school and get on with college. Even college might have seemed like an effort to get through. You finally made it to the finish line, glad that this chapter of your life is over. Now you just want the next phase of your life to begin.

It's hard to be patient as a child or teenager. While growing up, you're anxious for the next stage of your life to begin, a stage when you'll be more independent, when you won't have to answer to parents or teachers. Well, guess what? You're there! This is the moment you've been waiting for your entire life. You're finally an adult, and an accomplished one at that, with a college degree under your belt. Maybe best of all, you're in your twenties! Instead of stressing over who your new boss might be or where your career might lead you, remind yourself that you're young and vibrant. Your twenties are an exciting age! Within reason, you can go anywhere and do anything. Your mind and your lifestyle are more open now than they will ever be again. So enjoy it!

As you get older, your interests and tastes will change. Enjoy the things you can do now, both by yourself and with friends, that might seem out of place, as you get older—or that you probably won't have the time for later anyway.

That includes taking career chances. On a whim, send a letter or your resume to a company that you think would be fun to work for, even though you may have no experience. Many companies like taking on new, young, and energetic employees, especially at entry-level positions. Now is the time to experiment, before you have more important commitments than meeting your friends on a Friday night.

Enjoy being in your twenties. Don't stress about what might come later. Don't look anxiously to the future. There will be no other time like this in your life.

10.

Reflect Upon
Why You Might Be Indecisive

Not knowing what you want to do with yourself after college can be stressful. Along with the constant questions from family and friends is the more disturbing question you ask yourself: What do I want out of my life? And perhaps even more disturbing: How come I don't know what I want?

The only one who can answer that, of course, is you. Now that things have quieted down, now that those final exams are past and the graduation hoopla is over, it is the perfect opportunity to reflect on your indecisiveness.

Remember that you are not alone. Sure, some people come out of college and go straight into that dream job. They're on their way, their courses are set, and they seem to have the career compass pointing in the right direction. But not everyone starts running right out of the gate. Beginning a job right away is fine, but if you're still weighing your options, don't worry.

Weighing your options is a good thing. In some cases, a hasty career decision can turn out to be a disaster. Think of yourself as someone who wants to make the right decision rather than the quick decision.

Finally, think about your indecision, but don't stress about it. Consider all the things you enjoy now that you might have to give up if you were suddenly to start working a "real" job. Perhaps you actually enjoy your part-time job. Or maybe you enjoyed studying your major, but working in that field for the rest of your life seems daunting. Whatever your reasons for not knowing what you want to do, believe that they are good ones.

Most important of all, acknowledge your indecisiveness as a mode of self-exploration. If you look inward and reflect on who you are and what will make you happy, the time will be well spent, and it is excellent preparation for your future.

11.

Accept That You
Don't Know It All

You've just spent four years or more in an institute of higher learning. Mentally, you're armed with all sorts of theories, principles, and techniques just waiting to be put into action. Perhaps you've even participated in an internship program, gaining hands-on experience and a couple of letters of recommendation.

You're ready! Nothing can stop you!

Except for your own overconfidence.

One of the pitfalls many college graduates face is distorted expectations. Because they've just spent four years—and a lot of money—earning a degree, they feel that the job world should welcome them with open arms, willing to absorb the information they have learned and anxious to see common job practices from a new perspective.

However, college graduates often learn a startling lesson as they embark on their careers—they *don't* know it all. It's learning to accept this fact that makes dealing with what you don't know easier.

Let's face it—no one who is older wants to hear from some young pup, fresh out of college, how to do his or her job. And in most cases, a veteran employee does know more. The individual who has been in the field and worked in the trenches probably has a better handle on job responsibilities than someone just off the graduation runway.

As a college graduate, you have to accept that your first job will probably send you down to the bottom of the totem pole. Understand that you have a lot to learn and that, even with your college degree, you don't know it all. It can be a hard pill to swallow, but it doesn't have to be. From the outset, accept that you don't know it all. You can contribute a fresh perspective with deference and respect. More than likely, you will be thanked for your keen insight.

12.

Try Temping or Volunteering

Some believe that the most respectable thing to do right out of college is to get on the fast track to your career. If this happens for you, terrific! If not, or if you're going through the "I'm not sure what I want to do" blues, then why not consider temping or volunteering?

Temp agencies are an excellent way to get your feet wet in the work world. Of course, as a temp, you might be asked to do simple, mundane tasks, like inputting data or typing letters. However, many of these responsibilities are the same as those required of an entry-level employee.

As you temp, you'll also gain some valuable insight. You'll learn about office politics and get a feel for the working atmosphere of various companies. As you observe all of these aspects of a workplace, your own career goals might come into sharper focus. You'll realize which type of work you find most challenging. And of course, you'll be sharpening your skills, however menial your tasks may seem to you.

Another sound reason for temping is networking. Temping gets you into the workforce. By its very nature, it encourages you to meet people, to shake hands with executives, and to showcase your skills to a new company as the need arises.

Volunteering is another excellent way to get your foot in the door. The downside, of course, is that there is no payment involved. However, some industries that are hard to break into are sometimes open to hiring volunteers, looking to save money where they can.

Suppose you majored in environmental studies. The fish and wildlife department in your state might receive hundreds of applications, but they are always looking for volunteers. Offer your services. Work hard and make your presence known. Not only is the experience an excellent addition to your resume, but if a job opens up, you may leapfrog over all those applications.

So if the dream job hasn't come calling yet, consider temping or volunteering. Both are excellent ways to get your foot in the door and get hands-on job experience.

13.

Let Your
Friends Go

Y ou studied together, partied together, and maybe even lived together. Over the past four years, you developed meaningful friendships with people you imagine will always be a part of your life. That is why, when the time is right, you must let them go.

Friendships change, and as you begin your "real" life, things are going to come between you and your friends. It might not happen today or tomorrow, but eventually, you will drift apart. Jobs, marriage, kids, and changing lifestyles—these are all things that come between friends, no matter how close.

The issue, then, is how to deal with it. You can fight it every step of the way, insisting that you stick to your traditional routine of dinner and drinks every Friday night at the corner pub. Or you can accept that your friends—and you—will have more pressing things to attend to in the coming years. It doesn't mean that your friends or you care any less—only that you're all moving on.

There's nothing wrong with that. Although it might seem stressful to watch the gap between you and your once-closest pals widen, the stress is actually in trying to keep those friendships meaningful. You need to understand when your friends have to turn their attention more toward themselves, toward their own decisions and choices. And you will have to do it, too. Letting your friends go is hard, but trying to keep them around can be even harder.

14.

Take It Slow

College might have seemed like a whirlwind at times. As you look back, it probably seems like a blur of classes, cramming, and socializing. Now that you're done, you might find yourself still spinning around, ready to fly off in whichever direction the carousel happens to stop.

Slow down! Now is the time to jump off the carousel and let others ride around for a while.

One of the biggest pressures that might face you when you graduate is a sense of *immediacy*. You must know what you want *immediately*. You must have a future plan *immediately*. You must have your resume together *immediately*. You must have interviews lined up *immediately*.

Who made these rules? Why are these predestined tasks that you must accomplish the minute the college doors slam behind you?

The truth is that they're not. If you feel the need to slow down, do it. Okay, so your best friend is full of motivation, ready to take the world by storm and a career by the horns. Good for your friend! But if this is not you, that's fine. Taking it slow is a perfectly acceptable way to handle being a college graduate.

Remember, everyone marches to their own tune, but also at their own pace. Some people like to hit the ground running. But rest assured that there is no crime in taking it slow. Acknowledging what makes you the most comfortable is the first step.

Take your days after graduation at your own speed. You've just crossed one of the biggest finish lines of all and received the prize—your diploma. Now stretch your muscles and get ready for the next race. Once you get started, it will be hard to stop.

15.

Listen to Advice
with Grace

As a college graduate, you have your own ideas. The last thing you want to do is listen to a bunch of old-timers explain how they got started in life. "That was then, this is now," you think to yourself. "What do they know about living in today's world?"

Reacting this way every time a well-meaning family member or friend tries to offer you advice will do nothing but stress you out. Try not to do it. Believe it or not, it's much easier to smile and say thank you—and mean it—than to fake it and grumble to yourself. Your relatives don't mean to imply that you don't know what you're doing. They're only trying to help.

Friends offering advice can sometimes be just as annoying, especially if they started careers right after college. The implication is that if they could do it, then certainly you should be able to do it, too. Again, try not to react negatively. Getting defensive will cause anxiety all around.

Instead, the next time someone tries to offer advice, listen to it. In fact, as you nod agreeably, you might actually find a kernel of wisdom that you can use. Although people may be bombarding you with strategies and tactics for how to proceed now that you've graduated, you might actually learn something meaningful that can help you.

Listen with an open mind and a friendly heart. It sounds corny, but most of the people giving you advice have been there. They really might know what they're talking about. And don't forget to say thank you!

16.

Life Happens While
You're Waiting for It

The idea that life finally begins once you graduate from college is a popular misconception. Getting out of college is definitely a beginning, but not the beginning of your life. It is another phase of your life, and there will be many phases to live through.

As a college graduate, you need to keep in mind that life is what happens while you're waiting for life to "begin." Essentially, that means that just because you are out of college and waiting for the next stage to begin, you haven't stopped living. Therefore, you shouldn't let these days pass you by.

You're probably very aware that while you're waiting for your life to "begin," others are living what you'd consider fulfilling, meaningful lives of their own. Merely waiting around for something to happen to you is not only counterproductive, but also can be depressing.

Don't let this happen. Remember that you are in the midst of one of the most exciting times of your life. You are on the verge of discovering your path, whether you choose it or it chooses you. Try to fill your days with anticipation and awe, and look forward to the challenges you face each day. Even though you may feel as if you are in a holding pattern, your life is happening, right here, right now. Recognize that these days of transition are just as much a part of your life as landing a job and putting yourself on the career path.

Don't give yourself the added pressure of wishing those days were here now. Enjoy the moments that you're living in and make them productive.

17.

Fulfill a
Lifelong Dream

One of the ways to remember that your life is happening right now is to do something that you've always wanted to do. After all, when will you ever be in a position again where your time is your own?

A lifelong dream doesn't have to be travel-related. Perhaps you always wanted to offer your time to a humanitarian or environmental organization, but never had the chance. You do now! Or maybe you want to spend more time with your grandparents. Or perhaps you want to perfect your golf game. Now is the time!

The period between college graduation and starting a career is a unique one. As a college graduate, you are old enough and wise enough to enjoy new adventures, relax with friends and family, or give of yourself in interesting and altruistic ways. You are young enough to appreciate the newness of the experience.

One thing that leads to stress in life is missed opportunities. Wondering and wishing "If only I had done this," or "I wish I had done that" can make you feel unhappy or discontent. Don't give yourself the chance to wonder. Take this short break between college and the rest of your life to fulfill a lifelong dream. Not only will it give you something to cherish later in life, but it will help you get ready to move on to the career that's waiting for you.

18.
Keep Your Options Open

As graduation approached, you probably filled your mind with all sorts of things you had to do next, or even all sorts of things you would never do. For example, you might tell yourself to refuse any job for less than a certain salary; or you might insist that you will only accept a job in a particular sector.

However, putting such limitations on yourself not only narrows your options, but it creates an added burden. Now you are no longer just looking for a job. You are looking for *the* job. The job must fulfill all of your requirements, whatever those might be.

But what if that job just isn't available right now?

There is nothing wrong with outlining the criteria you want in a new job. These criteria will help mold your choices and guide you in the proper direction. However, these criteria can also become stifling and rigid if you refuse to consider other options.

It is important to be flexible. That doesn't mean you compromise on everything, although there's really nothing wrong with that, either.

What it means is that you consider the possibilities of a job that might not be exactly what you had in mind. Realize the possibilities. Imagine the experience you can gain that could ultimately aid in your noble endeavor to find the perfect job.

Removing boundaries from your search will alleviate the job-hunting pressure. Don't think of it as "selling out." View it more as not wanting to pass up an opportunity. Keep your options open, and more career choices will be available to you.

19.

Be Happy for the Friend
Who Lands That First Job

It's bound to happen. Someone you know well is going to "make it happen" before you do. Sure, you'll be happy for your friend, but deep down, some other emotions may arise. You may also feel jealous, guilty, and discouraged about your own job prospects.

All of these negative feelings are natural. But don't let this become about you. Instead of adding extra pressure to your life by wallowing in self-pity—and that's what it is—rise to the occasion, and be happy for your friend. Offer to buy your friend a drink or dinner. Not only will it make you feel better, but you can pump your friend for information, asking about the interview and his or her strategy for finally landing a job.

The best way to handle a friend's good news is to prepare for it. As college students, you probably had different successes in school, and you were happy for each other then. This should be no different. Be happy for your friend who gets that first job. Your first job is on the horizon, too.

20.

Ignore Those
Defensive Instincts

Up until this point in your life, you understood what was expected of you. Now that you've graduated, expectations can be wide and varied. Many will expect you to get a job. Or people may expect you to move out on your own. Perhaps your family expects you to go to graduate school.

The problem is that *you* don't know what you expect of yourself. It's a whole new ballgame, with you calling the shots instead of a parent or teacher. This might cause you to feel defensive. Now it's not others' expectations that are being challenged, but your own.

For example, you and your friend choose different paths; one of you gets right to work, and the other takes time off to travel. Neither of you should feel the need to defend your position, but it might feel like you do.

If you're happy with your decision, then comments from friends and family will merely roll off your back, like water off a duck.

Going on the defensive is like trying to convince yourself that you've made the right choice. In that event, you are second-guessing yourself.

Defensive instincts come to the forefront when you feel that you must justify your decisions to someone else. And that is simply not necessary. The only person you need to justify your decisions to is *you*. If you're comfortable with your decision, don't get defensive. Simply state, "I made the decision that was right for me," and leave it at that. Be confident in your own choices.

21.

Call a College Mate
to Commiserate

College is over and done with. It's time to move on. Part of you is relieved that graduation is behind you—but part of you also misses it just a tiny bit. After all, back then, you knew your place in the world. You were a college student! You were on the road to self-discovery, to making something of yourself.

Now you're on the superhighway of the rest of your life. It may be frightening, standing there and looking at the vast unknown of your life ahead. Where are the good old days? You might even welcome cramming for a physics exam if it meant that you didn't have to think about the uncertainty of the future.

If things are totally overwhelming you, call a friend from college. It just might surprise you to learn that your college mate feels exactly the same way. Even though you and your friends are very different people who experience changes in different ways, a college friend will still understand where you're coming from.

Commiserating with a friend has two positives. First, it allows you to lighten your emotional load. Expressing your doubts, fears, and concerns—saying them out loud—not only makes you feel better, but it gives those doubts less power over you. We have a tendency to blow things out of proportion in our minds. Voicing your fears out loud releases you. Suddenly, your worries might not seem as overpowering to you, and your friend will probably point out why they shouldn't be in the first place.

Commiserating with a friend allows your friend to vent his or her anxieties in return. Listening to other people who share the same feelings you do can help you realize that you're not alone. You're not the only one out of college who feels insecure, who has self-doubts, who wonders if he or she will ever really find a fulfilling job. In fact, you'll probably try to bolster your friend's own confidence, which in turn will help bolster your own.

Graduating from college is a huge change. Feeling a little apprehensive about the future is only natural. It helps to realize that you're not out there alone. Make a call.

22.

Write to Someone That You Admire

Many people influence our lives. They can be family or friends, college professors or current bosses—even athletes or entertainers. Who do you admire, and why? Now would be the perfect time to put your thoughts on paper. Write to someone that you admire.

This shouldn't be a fan letter. Think of it as more of an affirmation of your own goals and dreams; a way to keep yourself focused and remember what led you on the current path you've chosen for yourself.

Everyone we come in contact with affects us in some way. We may take little bits of a person and add them, however seamlessly, into our own personas. We may even see something in someone that we *don't* like and subconsciously knock out a habit we now realize we don't want.

However, try to focus on the positive. Perhaps a grandparent always wanted to be a lawyer and influenced you to go into law. Or maybe a college professor was instrumental in steering your major in the proper direction. Or maybe during an internship, someone became a mentor and taught you invaluable skills.

Perhaps you want to write to someone that you've never met, but whose career you've followed. Perhaps your favorite author inspired you to be a writer, or a favorite actor motivated you to major in theater. People we admire from a distance can be just as powerful in our lives as those we see on a regular basis.

Express how you feel. Describe the person's accomplishments and your hopes that someday your career may be similarly successful. Explain how advice given or choices made affected your own decisions. The letter doesn't have to be excessive—only to the point.

Reread your letter after you've finished writing it. Think about how your life has changed because of this person's role in it. Reflect on how your career choice was influenced by the things this person said or did. As you do so, you'll be reaffirming your reasons for achieving your degree and selecting your career.

Should you mail your letter? Well, that's up to you. The exercise is more of a personal one—it should not only be about the other person, but about you, too. If you feel comfortable sharing your thoughts, then go ahead and send it. If not, keep the letter in a drawer. When you begin to have doubts about your choices, reread your letter. It will help you remember your goals and dreams if they get lost in the post-graduation shuffle.

23.
Acknowledge Your
Strengths and Weaknesses

We all have strengths that we're proud of and weaknesses that we wish we could sweep under the carpet. For some, acknowledging strengths is easier than recognizing weaknesses. For others, it's the other way around. Understanding both is important as you graduate college, because once you acknowledge something, it will have less power over you, and therefore be less of a stress factor.

Fear of failure can cause us great anxiety. Sometimes when we know that we are weak in certain aspects of either our personalities or our skills, we tend to wait for those weaknesses to appear, alerting others to our faults.

First of all, you need to realize that you probably exaggerate your weaknesses. We tend to blow what we see as our shortcomings way out of proportion. Second, if you're aware of your weaknesses and acknowledge them outright—if you look them in the face—you'll be able to do something about them. Take another course.

Confide to a colleague or mentor the doubts you have about a certain ability. With a little bit of work, you can probably turn those weaknesses into stellar strengths.

For some people, acknowledging strengths can be just as daunting as facing weaknesses. You might feel that if you do so, you'll become overly confident, so you temper your feelings, downplaying your strengths and giving them equal footing with your weaknesses.

Acknowledging your strengths, however, does not mean that you should think that you do certain things better than anyone else. Acknowledging your strengths merely means that you know what you can do, and you do it well. Your strengths are what got you through college, and they are what will get you that first job. Your strengths will only grow stronger, while your weaknesses will grow weaker.

Stop stressing about your weaknesses. Acknowledge them and do something about them. Turn them into strengths, and apply them to all of the things that you can do for your future.

24.

Accept Your
Friends' Decisions

The college experience was something that brought you and your friends together. The lives that you choose afterward will definitely come between you. How you react to your friends' choices will leave a lasting impression on your friendships. No matter what your friends decide to do after graduation, don't argue about it. Be a supportive friend, and accept your friends' decisions.

It may not be easy. Sometimes it's a lot harder to bite your tongue than to say what you really want to say. For example, suppose your friend has decided to climb Mount Everest. All you see are the dangers. All your friend sees is the excitement. Do you think your friend will appreciate you bringing him or her down? Would you?

When a friend shares a decision with you, he or she is looking for one thing—support. Okay, so working on a sheep ranch in New Zealand might be a little out there. Getting married at the age of twenty-one may never be a decision you would make. But unless your friend asks you to talk him or her out of it, there's not much you can say to change his or her mind—and in the process, you will only damage the friendship.

That's not to say that you should idly sit by and watch what you consider to be a life-altering mistake. Explain that you're playing devil's advocate and that you just want to make sure that your friend has considered all the angles. If your friend still decides to go through with it, there's not much more you can do. Know that you've done what you felt was right, and then wish your friend good luck.

Everyone learns in his or her own way. If a friend's decision truly is the wrong one, he or she will find out soon enough. However, if it turns out to be the right one, think of how you may feel for having persisted in trying to talk your friend out of it. So don't. Besides, you have your own decisions to worry about! Being able to accept the choices your friends make is one more way to ease the stress of the days to come.

25.

Give Up Your
Antiestablishment Attitudes

College was a time of self-exploration and analysis. You not only questioned who you were and tried to define yourself, but you questioned society and the world as a whole. You may have crusaded for worthy causes, protested against government policies, or rallied behind antiestablishment viewpoints. You probably looked down on your elders as the people who messed up the planet, and vowed that you would never become part of that system—never don a suit, work nine to five, and listen to light rock. You felt as if you and your generation would change the system and show the world what really matters.

A noble thought!

However, what really matters right now is that you get on with your life. That doesn't mean that you have to give up your ideals—only that you have to learn to work within the system to make them happen.

You probably learned in college that there are certain times when you have to play by the rules. You had to attend classes and take exams in order to pass. You had to meet registration deadlines, or you'd miss the chance to sign up for classes.

Think of how much you'll be missing if you can't follow a few rules now. They're not even major ones! Put on a suit. Get a professional haircut. Downplay your taste in your personal jewelry. Be respectful and courteous during an interview. None of this means that you're joining the establishment. It only means that you're willing to work within the establishment to make it better.

Your nonconforming ways have helped shape the person that you are today. They have contributed to forming your attitudes, ethics, and goals for the future. Channel these qualities effectively, and you will gain what every young person wants: a career that allows you to contribute to society and has personal meaning for you, as well.

26.

Feel Comfortable
Asking for Advice

O kay, so you might not have been ready to hear advice at the time, but now you are. The only problem is that you don't know how to go about getting it. The solution is really quite simple: Ask for it!

After graduation, there are so many things to consider. How do you set up your resume? Where should you go to look for a job? How should you handle yourself during an interview? What will interviewers ask, and how should you answer? Do you need to write thank-you notes after each interview? The questions keep coming.

The answers, however, don't have to lie only within you. Alleviate the burden and the stress by asking for advice. So many people around you have probably been where you are now: older friends, a current boss at a part-time job, brothers, sisters, cousins, college professors, counselors—and of course, don't forget your parents. Although they all might have different careers and arrived at them through different avenues, they all have one thing in common—they will love giving you advice.

So ask for it, even if you previously turned them down. Asking for advice is not so much an admission that you need help as an acknowledgement that others may have more experience in certain areas than you do. Those who have graduated from college, who went through the ups and downs after graduation and slogged through the job-finding process, are definitely one step ahead of you here.

Think of it this way: Writing a paper in school required you to do research. You used a number of sources, digging for information until you felt comfortable enough about the topic to write about it. Then you may have sat down and outlined your paper, noting the facts you found and setting up a guide to follow. The same method applies here. It's hard to leap right in when you don't know where to start. All the options swirling around your brain will leave you stressed out and exhausted.

So invite someone to share the burden. Ask people for advice. Look at the advice-givers as resources, helping you accumulate enough facts so that you can put a plan into action. Asking for advice is a small thing that can lead to much bigger results. Don't be afraid to ask for it. Remember—people love to share their expertise, and they love to feel needed. Not only will you be helping yourself, but you'll be making someone else feel good in the process.

27.

Realize That You Won't Always
Agree with Friends and Family

The sticky part of asking for and listening to advice is knowing that you won't always agree with the advice that is offered. In fact, you might not agree with a lot of the things your family and friends say right now. Instead of getting angry or ignoring them, you need to realize that you will see things differently than others, and then let go of those disagreements.

It's a fact of life. You and your parents may never see eye to eye on anything. They might not like your friends, they might not agree with the degree you chose to study, and they might not even agree with your goals and dreams. And no matter how much you argue with them about some things, they may never see them your way. This is the nature of the relationship between parents and kids. Your parents want what they feel is best for you. They don't want their kid to make the same mistakes they may have made. As they argue and discuss things with you, try to keep in mind that they are only being disagreeable out of love.

You, on the other hand, might have ulterior motives for disagreeing. Perhaps you feel that you can never agree with your parents, no matter the issue. This might be your way of asserting yourself, of proving to your parents that you are a viable adult with your own viewpoints, not a child who goes along with whatever they say.

Where friends are concerned, you might pose arguments for similar reasons. You may argue over the best way to approach job-hunting because you want your friends to recognize how creative and clever you are. You may choose to argue over the merits of sending out resumes through the Internet instead of via snail mail, just because you don't want them to think you've jumped on the technology bandwagon. What you're really doing is pushing your friends away.

You and your friends may disagree, as you may disagree with your family. However, just because you might not agree with their advice or choices doesn't mean you have to point out the errors of their ways and argue a point into the ground. Having your own opinions on how to proceed after college is fine—as long as you view others' ideas with the same respect that you'd like them to view yours.

28.

Networking Begins at Home

You've probably heard the old adage, "It's not what you know, but who you know." Essentially, this means that all your talent and skill won't get you in the door if someone isn't there to open it for you. Knowing someone in your chosen profession gives you an advantage over all of those faceless unknowns.

Of course, you might rebel against this notion. You might think, "I'm creative! I have talent! I can outshine anyone, including the niece or nephew of the CEO!"

The problem is that you may never get the chance. People feel comfortable working with others that they know or know of. Through recommendations, references, or even a friend of a friend, hiring for a position is much easier when an employer knows something about a future employee, rather than trying to decipher who someone is from a resume.

The best place to look for those connections is right under your own roof. Whether you live with your family or with roommates, ask if they know anyone in your field. You might explain that you're not necessarily looking for an interview, but perhaps just a knowledgeable professional who might be willing to point you in the right direction. From that one meeting, anything could happen.

This true story is a case in point. A college graduate was looking for a job in publishing. She took the typing tests, took the copyediting tests, and did a round of interviews, but after several months, she still came up empty-handed. Her roommate, knowing the field she was trying to enter, suggested that she talk to someone he knew, a friend of his mother's who had been in publishing for twenty-five years. The two met over lunch and had a nice conversation. Several months later, still on the job hunt, our college graduate received a call from her roommate's mother's friend. Her assistant had just quit. Did she want the job?

Listen to the connection again: the graduate's roommate's mother's friend! Sounds fairly convoluted, doesn't it? And perhaps almost impossible. But it's true.

The people around you are your best resources for networking and making connections. Maybe your father doesn't know anyone in banking, but a colleague's wife might. Maybe your brother doesn't know anyone in architecture, but his new girlfriend's cousin is a designer. You just never know, and you won't know if you don't ask.

Getting a job without having a few strings pulled is a noble idea, but it's not very realistic. If the opportunity arises to be introduced to someone in your field, jump on it. Getting your foot in the door will then be one less thing you have to worry about.

29.

Aim for
Your Dream Job

Your parents tell you that you're being foolish. Your friends exclaim, "No way!" Even your college professor, the one who encouraged you all along, has doubts. You've explained your dream job—what you ultimately want to accomplish—to each and every one of them. Perhaps you want to be a fashion designer in New York; or get a job in international banking overseas; or even work in the front office of your favorite sports team. Everyone sadly shakes their heads and says, "You're such a dreamer. Do you know how many people apply for jobs like that?"

True. But maybe just as many people have friends and family around them who talk them out of striving for their dream jobs. You don't have to be one of them.

The old motto, "Nothing ventured, nothing gained," is quite accurate here. And so is "You never know if you don't try." Send your resume to the CEO of the company that you desperately want to work for. If you want to combine your public relations degree with your favorite pastime, like baseball, find the number of the administrative office and give a call.

Even if you seem to get no positive responses, take a step backward and try again with the goal of slowly working your way up. If the New York Yankees front office didn't grant you an interview, try a minor league team. If that international banking corporation sent you an impersonal rejection letter, take it down a notch and try a slightly smaller company.

The point is not to lose sight of your dream job. Keep your eye on the target. Don't sweat it if you don't get there right out of college. You will get there eventually.

Don't let others try to talk you out of it, either. They may not understand what drives you, but at least you know. Think of how much more stressful it could be to be stuck at a job you truly dislike, always thinking, "I wish I had tried to work for so-and-so."

Sure, your dream job might be one that is wanted by hundreds of other people. Your enthusiasm and your energy can set you apart. Your excitement about working in your dream job will probably come through in your cover letter. And who would *you* rather hire—someone who is merely answering an ad, or someone who truly has a passion for the job?

Don't let the nay-sayers get to you. The only thing standing between you and your dream job is *you*. Go for it!

30.

Set Life and Job Priorities

Life can seem pretty confusing right after college. Friends are scattering around the state or country, getting jobs. Your family is constantly hounding you to get off your butt and do something with your degree. Or maybe you jumped right into a job, and you've started your career, full steam ahead. You may not have had a moment to regroup and analyze where you're going, much less if you're on the right track.

No matter where you are after graduation, it helps to list your priorities for both your job and your life. Knowing what's important to you and recognizing what you need to stay happy and fulfilled will lessen the stress of wondering if you're really doing the right things. Instead of getting bogged down by inconsequential details, figure out what really matters to you, and concentrate on those things, pushing the smaller ones to the sidelines.

For example, suppose maintaining the relationship with your boyfriend or girlfriend is really important to you. However, somehow you find yourself caught up in a wave of job socializing. Happy hours with new colleagues, weekend outings with work friends, long lunches that lead to extra hours at night—are these the things that really matter to you? Can you see who's getting lost in the shuffle?

Possibly, you don't. In your mind, you're advancing your career. You're making contacts. However, in the long run, your relationship suffers, and the one person who always meant the most to you may not be around much longer.

If outside influences are getting in your way, then you need to consider what is most important to you at this time. Write up a list of things that are important, not only in your personal life, but in your professional one, as well. Perhaps personally, you want to make sure that you always have time to volunteer at the Y. Putting it down on paper won't ensure that you'll stick to it, but it will make it more real. Perhaps you have a definite series of steps that you want to accomplish in your career. List them. You might have to be flexible, but at least you won't lose sight of your goals.

Setting down life and job priorities need not be confining. It only helps to reinforce what you already know—what is most important to you.

31.

Subscribe to a Magazine
in Your Field

While in school, you probably felt that you were learning a lot about your profession. The knowledge of theories, practices, and histories surely made you an expert in your field.

All this education is great, of course, but essentially what you gained was book knowledge. What you need now is real-world knowledge. What, exactly, is going on in your field? What are the latest trends? Who are the movers and shakers? Which companies are on the cutting edge, and which companies are in trouble?

Trying to figure all this out on your own can be nerve-wracking. Your textbooks probably aren't current enough to have such information. Approaching your career as suggested by an out-of-date resource is not a good way to go. Even the Internet can only help you so far. In order to find what you need on the Web, you need to have the essential information to plug into a search engine. So the question still remains—where do you begin?

Most professional fields have magazines that focus on their industry's needs and outlooks. Professional magazines are an ideal source to help you explore your career of choice up close, without actually having a job. Along with articles about the field, such magazines often have calendars of events, company updates, and even job listings.

Professional magazines are also a great source for contacts. These magazines often include announcements about the latest comings and goings in the industry. With the name in hand of the new person in charge of a department you'd like to work in, you can send a letter and resume directly to him or her. Not only does this show that you know your employer, but it also demonstrates knowledge of the field. This could be another detail that puts you above other applicants.

So take away the guesswork of trying to figure out the real nuts and bolts of your field. Subscribe to a professional magazine. You'll be getting the same insights as others who have been in the business for years.

32.

Ignore Forecasts
About the Job Market

Just as it is hard for meteorologists to predict the weather, it is difficult for financial forecasters to predict what the job market will be like. The best thing you can do when news reports—or even friends and family who claim to be "in the know"—come out with predictions about the job market is to ignore them.

The most obvious job-market forecast to be worried about is a bad one. You might hear things such as: "The market is glutted with computer technicians." "There aren't enough law firms to hire all of the lawyers coming out of college." "Business majors are going to have a tough time because of corporate downsizing." It couldn't get any more discouraging.

Don't let it. "Experts" aren't always right. These are their ideas; they are often based on historical statistics, which allow them to try to predict where the current trend is headed. And they could be wrong, just like a weather person can be wrong. Basically, when these forecasters are telling you where they think the job market stands, they're just telling you their opinions. You might already have doubts about finding a job in your field, so why add to them? Sweep those predictions under the carpet, and continue on in your search.

Positive job forecasts can be problematic, too. Upon hearing that there are plenty of jobs in a particular field, you might sway your cover letter to reflect a certain relevant skill. Your focus may turn from getting a job you really want to getting just any job.

Another problem with a positive job forecast is expectation. The "experts" might be swooning about all the jobs available in a field such as advertising, for example. Surely, you shouldn't have a problem finding a job if this was your major. But what if you do have trouble with your job search? Quickly, you'll become discouraged, rationalizing that with so many jobs out there, you must be at the bottom of the barrel if you can't get one.

Job-market forecasts can be interesting to listen to, but take them in stride—don't let them either upset or elate you. Stay on your path, with your direction clear and your outlook positive.

33.

Take Advantage of
Job Resources at School

Probably, the last place you feel like returning to right now is school. After all, you've moved on. You've put college behind you. What could school possibly have to offer that you didn't get the first time around?

Well, the first time around, you were focused on different things. You were concentrating on passing classes, taking exams, signing up for internships, and socializing. You didn't have time or even the motivation to think beyond the school week, much less beyond graduation. But that time has finally come and gone. Now school can offer you something else. It is one of the great places to look for job opportunities.

Start by checking with the department of the subject of your major. Oftentimes, the main office will have a display with current job openings posted in your field. If you don't see anything, ask. Sometimes counselors or assistants have knowledge of jobs in different areas.

Talk with your college professors. You might not have had time to talk with them during school because of the demands placed on both of you. Revisit your school, or contact a college professor by phone. Explain your dilemma. Your professors will be glad to offer advice and have ideas on how to get started.

One final place to look is in the internship department of your college. Internships are arranged in conjunction with a variety of companies. This affords you more names and places to send your resume—and you already know that the company has shown an interest in hiring or using college students.

One of the things you should try to do now that you are out of school is to minimize. Minimize your stress. Minimize the pressure of looking for a job. Minimize the anxiety of not knowing where to begin. One of the easiest ways to do that is to go back to something familiar. Go back to school, and take advantage of their resources. You might be surprised by what you find.

34.

Don't Obsess Over
What Goes on Your Resume

The time comes when every college graduate is faced with a grim reality—the writing of the resume. Admittedly, your resume is important to anyone who might want to give you a job— it's a list of skills and accomplishments that you've achieved in your field.

Think about what makes you proud when you look back over your college career. What classes did you excel in? What projects did you ace? What extracurricular activities did you participate in that show your versatility and willingness to work hard?

Write all of these things down. You might not want to put them all on your resume, but seeing them in a list will make you realize how much you have to say about yourself.

Putting the resume together can be stressful because you may feel that it is a reflection of you. Many thoughts probably go through your mind as you draft your resume: "What image will people have of me from reading this? What picture am I painting of myself? Would I grant me an interview if I saw my resume?"

The answer to all of these questions is simple—you really don't know. Viewing a resume is a subjective process, just like watching a movie or reading a book. People are all different, so they come away with different impressions and ideas. You're not going to be able to second-guess the resume reader.

Once you stop second-guessing, you can stop worrying about your resume. Write down what you feel are your best accomplishments and skills—those that really stand out—and know that it's the best you can do. It will be enough.

35.

Hire Someone to Design
Your Resume for You

Another way to ease any resume anxiety is to have someone design your resume for you. With a personal computer, anyone can set up and design a resume, complete with different typefaces, colors, and other interesting features. But unless you have a talent for desktop publishing, figuring out how to set up and determine what looks right can be frustrating or time-consuming. You may want to consider hiring someone to do it for you.

Many local print shops can design a resume for you. Simply bring in a handwritten resume, and they'll type it up, make margins even, make columns align, and take care of all the other intricacies that can be difficult. A print shop will also probably be able to make the resume as fancy or as plain as you like. The shop will probably have a book of samples that you can look through to help you pick out the right style.

Unless you're going into a creative field like advertising or graphic arts, a traditional, standard resume form is just fine. After all, imagine you are a person in human resources, looking through dozens of resumes. Do you want to have to figure out some strange new resume presentation, or would you rather just view the normal, traditional style, knowing where all the information is supposed to be? Instead of catching someone's idea with your originality, you might just be finding your way to the trash can if you make your resume too difficult to read.

Stick with the tried and true, and let someone else do the "dirty" work. Let someone else make sure your name is centered, that the lines aren't cut off at the bottom, and that it all looks neat and simple and easy to read.

You must proofread your resume before it goes to print. A second glance can't hurt, and it may save you from an embarrassing error. Remember, even though someone else is designing and printing your resume, you are ultimately responsible for what's on it.

36.

Research Jobs and
Companies in Your Field

As a college graduate, there are so many opportunities available to you. In some professions, the choices may seem virtually limitless. Which companies should you send your resume to? What jobs should you be applying for? Such questions can bog you down, especially if jobs are plentiful. The best way to start is to do a bit of research.

For example, suppose you look in the paper for job listings in the field of marketing. Dozens of jobs are listed, and you meet most of the requirements. Your mind starts to spin. How do you differentiate between them? How do you determine if the jobs and companies meet *your* requirements?

At the beginning of your job search, you may want to explore the Internet sites for companies in your field to find out what each of them has to offer. Then make a list of the companies you would most like to work for. Analyze your list. Think about the features of these companies that make them special to you. Is it the fact that the companies are based near home? Do they have a long and steady tradition? Are they new and on the cutting edge? What, exactly, are the requirements that make a company one that you'd like to join?

Next, look at the available positions. Although you should keep your options open, getting just any job in your desired company is not going to do the trick. If you really want to be an editorial assistant for a magazine, working in the accounting department is probably not the right move for you. Make sure that the job offers what you want—and what you need—to be happy and fulfilled.

Researching jobs and companies will help you shorten the list of places to send your resume, and it will help you weed out multiple job listings and job offers. If you are lucky enough to be able to pick and choose the job that you want, you need to feel secure in your decision. Knowing what you require in a job or company—looking at the company's "resume," in a manner of speaking—will ease some of your doubts and worries.

37.

Explore the Internet

Sometimes it's hard to remember what the world was like before the Internet. So much information is available, literally at the tips of our fingers. Using the Internet and the information you can find there can take a great burden off your shoulders.

Before the Internet, the only way to really find out about a company was to visit, call, or send away for a brochure (unless an industry magazine just ran an article on a company of interest). Getting detailed information about a company—its history, its hiring practices, its mission statement—was extremely time consuming.

The Internet has changed all that. As more and more companies make official web sites, you can find a lot of what you'd like to know online. A company web site may contain descriptions of company products, a message from the president, quotes from satisfied customers, explanations of recent happenings—even a list of job openings. The Internet is an amazing way to find information quickly.

You can also find out what others say about a prospective company. Run a web search using the company name. See what comes up. You might find sites that have newspaper articles, information on other companies it's involved with, or related web sites. The point is to have as much information at your disposal as possible so that you can make job decisions without fretting about them.

A number of headhunting companies have cropped up online. Post your resume at their sites, and employers can view the resumes for possible job candidates. Other web sites list jobs for which you can post your resume. You may also find information about hot companies that are hiring. Some sites even have a special "college grads" section of advice and tips for job searches.

Surfing the 'Net has become an indispensable way of gaining information. If you have a computer and the Internet is available to you, use it as a resource to aid your job-hunt.

38.

Appearance Is
Important—for Confidence

How many of you hate to be reminded, "First impressions are lasting impressions"? Unfortunately, this adage holds true for most employers. Unfortunately for you, it means that your appearance really does count. It seems clichéd and very establishment, but it's a fact of job-hunting. The right outfit will not necessarily get you the right job, but it will make an interviewer sit up, take notice, and listen to you with respect. Listening in such a manner, the person sitting on the opposite side of the desk from you will have a better chance of admiring what you've achieved and acknowledging that you have skills and talents that can be an asset to the company or business.

There is an added bonus here, as well. If you've taken the time to care about your appearance, you will feel good. Feeling good gives you confidence. Confidence allows you to speak clearly and succinctly. It helps you express your ideas with enthusiasm. When you feel confident, you make others feel confident in their decision to hire you. That doesn't mean that you should be *over*confident. Don't saunter into an interview with an air of, "Why wouldn't you hire me? I'm terrific." Step with a sure foot, not an arrogant stroll.

You want your interview outfit to express a little bit about who you are; yet at the same time, you need to show that you're the right professional for the job. You definitely don't want to have to worry about your clothes in the middle of an interview. Get a grip on your wardrobe ahead of time.

And if you realize after an interview that your scarf or tie was crooked, or even that you had food stuck between your teeth—so what? That little inconsistency might just make you more memorable. Keep your clothes simple and comfortable. Feel good about how you look, and you'll feel good about the interview.

39.

Understand That
Being Nervous Is Okay

There's no way to get around it. Interviews are a drag. Job interviews will probably be some of the most stressful events that you'll go through after graduation. Before an interview, you begin psyching yourself up—yet the whole thing may terrify you. You may begin to think that your whole future rests on this meeting.

Understand that it's okay to be nervous. Everyone who goes through the interview process is nervous. Not knowing what to expect has that effect, especially when you believe that so much is riding on your performance. It's comparable to an audition. Realize that in feeling this way, you're not abnormal or even atypical.

During the interview, it is hard not to weigh each and every word you say. You'll wish you could see yourself from the interviewer's perspective. But remember, all the little things that bother you are probably only obvious to you. In your mind, you're building up all sorts of tiny faults and miscues. Take a deep breath, and just let the interview happen. After all, you're not in the driver's seat—the interviewer is. The interviewer sets the pace and asks the questions. Follow this person's lead, and take the stress off your own shoulders.

Don't spend time after the interview criticizing every imaginary thing that you perceive you said or did wrong. Did you shake the interviewer's hand firmly enough? Did you smile too much or not enough? Did you exude all manner of confidence and integrity? Did you answer each question properly?

These details, which seem catastrophic to you, are *minor*. An interviewer is looking at the total package, not nitpicking at details like you are. You will probably be nervous before, during, and after an interview, so try not to let the smaller things stress you out.

40.

Put the First Interview
Behind You

Experiencing anything for the first time is always tough, and that goes for interviews. The biggest problem with the first interview is that you probably don't know what to expect.

Hopefully, your first interview will not be quite as frightening as you imagine. Nerve-wracking, yes. Intimidating, without a doubt. But not a complete washout.

Okay, well, maybe it does turn out that way.

No matter how your interview goes, put it behind you. You might spend *some* time analyzing it. Pick apart your answers, your gestures, and your mannerisms. Try to figure out what an interviewer's cryptic comment might have meant, or what answer he or she was really fishing for.

Then heave a sigh of relief, and drop it.

Interviews are a learning process, and like most things, they take practice to do well. If you feel that you have stumbled through an interview, learn from it. If you found that you got incredibly thirsty and could barely speak a word, the next time, you'll make sure you have a drink of water first. If you are unhappy with the way you phrased an answer, rest assured that you'll do better at the next interview.

Instead of dwelling on the woes and mishaps of your first interview, why not celebrate? Treat yourself to something nice, like dinner out with friends. After all, being able to get the interview meant that you did accomplish something—a prospective employer read your resume and found it to be interesting enough to give you an interview! You've taken the first step. So celebrate, even if you don't end up with the job. There will soon be others for you to choose from.

41.

Concentrate on the
Positive Comments from an Interview

After an interview, you should take away with you anything positive that the interviewer might have said. If negative comments and impressions should be viewed as small things to forget about, then positive comments should be viewed as gifts to save and treasure.

Interviewers have no reason to say nice things to you. It sounds rather blunt, but it's true. So if an interviewer compliments you on your resume or points out an accomplishment that caught his or her eye, run with it! If the interviewer nods in approval at one of your answers, mentally pat yourself on the back. You did a good job.

Believe it or not, interviewers can sometimes be just as nervous as you, especially if the process is new to them. For example, suppose someone has just been promoted and has been asked to hire an assistant. He or she might be worried about how you will perceive him or her! A positive comment from you could just do the trick. Such comments don't have to sound like you're trying to score points (but of course you are, and the interviewer knows it). But a comment like, "This seems like such a nice company. You must be happy working here," not only invites the interviewer to talk about the company, but it provides a compliment, as well.

During the interview, accept compliments graciously. Afterward, focus on these positives and how you can make them stand out when you go through your next interview. Congratulate yourself on making a good impression. Pretty soon, the positive comments will begin to outweigh the negative comments in your mind. This in turn will boost your confidence and get you ready for whatever the next interview has in store.

42.

Know That Job Openings
Always Come Up

You've put the first interview behind you. You've focused on the positives instead of the negatives. Now comes the difficult stage—waiting for the phone to ring to hear the words on the other end: "We'd like to offer you the job."

But what happens if several days pass, and then an ominous-looking letter arrives in the mailbox with the company's logo? It's not so much that the letter looks bad, but that it looks impersonal. That can only mean one thing—you didn't get the job.

This is a very difficult pill to swallow. Even though you may have had your doubts about the success of the interview, you were probably still hoping to land the position. You may have told yourself not to get your hopes up, but deep down, you were truly hoping that you had made a good enough impression to get your foot in the door.

The worst thing you can do at this point is to become discouraged and believe that this job was the only one for you. It may take several interviews before you finally get offered a job. Although you may feel as if it is a reflection on you, turn the mirror around—it's a reflection of the interviewer. An interviewer likes to hire people he or she feels comfortable with. The rationale is that if the interviewer bonded with someone during an interview, then the working relationship will be easier. It makes sense. In any case, you shouldn't want to work with someone who may have felt that you didn't bond with him or her.

You also have to realize that just because that one job got away from you doesn't mean that the next one will. Jobs open up all the time. You might even have your next interview lined up already, only you were hoping you would have to cancel. (One interview was stressful enough, thank you!)

Going on more than one interview is really par for the course. If you were to talk to a dozen people, they could probably tell you their own horror stories about going on interviews, the jobs that they didn't get, and the ones that they did. Don't think of it so much as "the job that got away." Just tell yourself, "The next opportunity will be even better."

43.

Explore Life Changes
and Relocating

Finally, the call you've been waiting for has come. The company you really wanted to work for, your first choice, has offered you a job. The salary is good, and the benefits sound excellent. There's only one catch: The company wants you to relocate a thousand miles away.

The only person who can decide what to do is you. But you shouldn't let the prospect of relocating discourage or confuse you. Life changes. Life after college is about change. Your lifestyle will change, your priorities will change, your friends will change—why not the scenery, too? View relocating as just one more change to add to the interesting course your life is taking.

To start your new life, a change of scenery might actually be just the thing you need. It takes away the temptation to remain stagnant, to become placid and lose your motivation. A change of scenery can invigorate you and get you excited about the changes ahead.

Look at change as an adventure. Do you remember those first few days of college, four or five years ago? You were nervous and apprehensive, but you were also excited. You were about to embark on a new life, with all the possibilities of college spread out before you. The chance to relocate could be an adventure, too. Don't get bogged down by the details and the hassles of having to move. Think of the new city you'll get to know intimately, the new friends you'll meet, and the new job opportunities that will come your way.

What's great about relocating is that you're not out there by yourself. Your company is like a safety net. In most cases, they will pay your moving expenses and hire a real estate agent to help you find an apartment, so you'll already be set up with a place to live. Also, you'll meet new people through your job. Even though you may be moving away from family and friends, you won't be out there all by yourself.

Perhaps one of the best reasons to consider relocating is because it's not just an opportunity—it's a golden opportunity. It's your chance to set out on your own, to make a name for yourself, to put your degree to work and meet the challenges of life head-on. Don't let the small details of relocating scare you off. Take the opportunity, and run with it!

44.

Treat Yourself When
You Land Your First Job

Congratulations! You did it! After all the sweating, wondering, soul-searching and job-hunting, you finally landed your first job after college. What are you waiting for? Treat yourself to something special!

So often, we reward ourselves when negative things happen. We pig out on ice cream when we're upset. We go on shopping sprees to make ourselves feel better. We indulge our whims when we get depressed.

You also need to reward yourself when positive things happen, and landing your first job is definitely a positive! So treat yourself! If eating ice cream makes you feel happy, buy your favorite flavor. If buying a bunch of CDs floats your boat, then load up the CD rack. If driving down to the beach sounds like the perfect ending to a perfect day, then do it!

Rewarding yourself is not being selfish. Acknowledging that you've earned a reward is merely that—telling yourself that you did a good job. As you treat yourself, the small, troublesome details that seemed to be insurmountable just a few days ago will disappear.

Movie stars win Academy Awards for jobs well done. Athletes win Most Valuable Player trophies. Well, you are your most valuable player, and you need to let yourself know that. Wallow in your positive achievement. Enjoy it for all it's worth. You deserve it!

45.

Take Your Parents
Out to Dinner

Your parents have seen you through thick and thin. Many times, they've supported you, and perhaps just as many times, they've wondered if your head was screwed on right. Well, now is not only the time to thank them for all they've done, but to share your success with them, especially if you have been at odds over your college and career choices.

No matter how your parents may act toward you, parents want their children to succeed, and they want their children to be happy. Unfortunately, what they think will make you happy isn't always the same thing that you think will make you happy.

Put aside those differences, at least for one meal. Taking your parents out to dinner is a way to celebrate, but it's also a way to show your parents that you've made it. It's a way to say, "Look at me! I've done it! You can feel proud! I am about to enter the job force and be a fairly responsible adult."

If you have a good relationship with your parents, such a dinner will not be a great hardship. If you and your parents have always been at odds, take this opportunity to put those differences aside. For one night, let the bad feelings go. Tell your parents about your interview experiences, share funny anecdotes about the people you've met so far, and impress them with what your job responsibilities will be. Your parents want to be proud of you. Inviting them out to dinner—at your expense—will make them feel doubly so.

Express your appreciation. Let them know that you realize all that they've done, and now you'd like to give a little back to them. After a night of pleasant discussion around a good meal, perhaps the huge differences between you might not seem quite so vast after all.

46.

Embrace the
Entry-Level Job

Although you are now a college graduate, you still have a lot to learn. To think that you are a shoo-in for any job, regardless of your past achievements and efforts, is misguided.

One college graduate learned after going on several interviews that a prospective employer felt college graduates weren't willing to start out at the bottom. He felt that despite a lack of credentials, young people without degrees were more willing to pay their dues.

How's that for a reality check? This interviewer was implying that people without college degrees are willing to work in the trenches, whereas college graduates, with all their classes and degrees, are not.

Embrace your first job. In most cases, it will be an entry-level position. That means you'll be at the bottom of the corporate totem pole, most likely as someone's assistant. Don't gripe about typing letters or sending faxes. Your boss knows you want to do more. Your boss is aware of your degree and your skills, and will give you a chance to show what you can do—after you've proven yourself. After all, if you can't handle the routine, mundane tasks of the job, how are you supposed to take on bigger responsibilities?

No matter how boring the tasks may be, try to view them as part of the learning process, as stepping stones that will lead to greater heights. Think about it. If you were a boss, would you entrust an important ad campaign to someone you barely knew, or would you allow an assistant who has proven to be responsible and trustworthy a chance to share insights and strategies?

Once you get a job, your degree and your resume no longer speak for you. How you perform on the job does. Make the most of it. Don't grumble about doing the small things that are important to the daily grind.

47.
Let Go of
One College Pastime

Your life is changing. Whether you're ready for it or not, whether you want it to change or not, your life right now is in perpetual motion, and not much remains constant. You might be tempted to try to hang on to as much of your college life as possible. After all, college made you feel alive. You explored yourself, the world, and your options. You reached your peak as an individual and began to define yourself. Why would you want to give any of that up?

However, there is a time to move on for all of us, and holding on to pastimes that you enjoyed once can start to become stressful. How can doing what you enjoy be stressful? Right now, with your life changing and gears switching, you might not really have the time or the energy for your favorite pastime. If you're working nine to five, hanging out with your buddies every Thursday night might be harmful to your performance at work on Friday. If you and your friends always go golfing on Sundays, you might find yourself too drained to tackle work again on Monday. Trying to maintain your old lifestyle can become not only a drag, but a burden.

Try giving up one thing. Realize that missing one pastime is not really that big a deal, especially with everything else you have going on in your life. Your friends might not understand, but eventually they will, because they will have to give something up, too.

Attempting to hold on to a lifestyle or a pastime that no longer fits into your life can be exhausting. You're straddling two worlds— your new professional life and your college days. At this point in time, you need to concentrate on your new responsibilities. That's not to say that you should never party with your friends again or hang out at the old stomping grounds. Just pass it up every once in a while. In the long run, you'll enjoy your pastimes much more when you participate on your own terms and your own time than when you join in out of tradition or obligation.

48.

Leave Your
Baseball Cap at Home

It's the night before your first day on the job. You're excited. You're anxious. You wonder what it will be like. You're trying to put your clothes together and thinking about the kind of impression you want to make. Who do you want people to see? Do you want them to see a young professional, ready to tackle the challenges of the workday? Or do you want them to see a college graduate with an attitude, ready to take on anyone who challenges him or her?

What you wear on your first day, of course, depends on your job. If you're working out in the field for the National Park Service, a business suit may not be necessary. If it's your first day teaching kindergarten, comfortable shoes are probably the right choice. If you're working for a hip, young magazine, then casual clothes may be more in order.

A good strategy for the first day of any job, though, is to dress conservatively. Test the waters. The last thing you want on your first day is for people to stare at you disapprovingly. Take your cues from others. See what everyone else is wearing on the job. After the first week or so, you'll be more able to commit yourself to a daily style.

Call attention to yourself with your work, with your clever ideas, and with your stunning insights—but play it cool in the clothing department during the first few days. Leave the baseball cap and T-shirt behind. Forget the sneakers this time, and wear shoes instead. Then your clothes will be one less thing you have to agonize over.

49.

View the First Day
on the Job as an Adventure

When you were in college, you probably loved to experiment with new experiences and new ideas. You viewed anything new and different as an adventure. Well, you're going to need that sense of adventure now more than ever. You're about to embark on a truly thrilling endeavor—your first job, maybe even your dream job.

Okay, so perhaps it's not an adventure in the sense that hang-gliding in Hawaii would be. But why not view it that way? Try to turn your nervous energy about your first day into excited energy. Be ready to absorb all that you're about to encounter.

No matter what job you take, you are about to make new discoveries. Perhaps you will learn how to run the monster-sized copy machine or learn how to interpret your boss's instructions. You may have to figure out how to navigate the hallways, or try to steer clear of a pack of gossiping coworkers. View them all as parts of the adventure, as highlights of your new voyage of discovery.

Don't let the details of your first day stress you out. Accept that you're not going to be able to see or do it all in one day. Accept that this adventure is going to take time to get used to. Don't worry if you miss a few things along the way. You'll pass by them again.

Hopefully, you'll never view your job in a ho-hum way, but you definitely don't want to start out like that on day one. The adventure has just begun!

50.

Take Notes When
Learning a New Task

Face it and accept it: Many of the responsibilities you'll be asked to take on in your entry-level job will seem fairly brainless. It doesn't take a genius to fill out a mailing slip. It doesn't take a rocket scientist to input data on a computer. You don't have to be Albert Einstein to figure out how to send a fax.

During your first few days on the job, you'll be bombarded with instructions and information. You'll learn how to do this, how to process that, who this form gets sent to, and what the sequence is for saving files. It may never occur to you that you could forget how to do these things. It seems so easy. You have a college degree, after all.

However, you also have a lot of stuff being thrown at you all at once. Did you ever enter a tough class and come unprepared, without a notebook and pen? You shouldn't enter your boss's office or a training session without these, either. The best way to learn on the job is the same way that you learned in school—take notes.

When someone comes over to show you how to log on to the company computer, write down the steps. Even though you're positive you'll never forget them, by the time you learn how to run the fax machine, the printer, and whatever other machines are at your workplace, you just might get the steps mixed up. If you write them down, you'll have instructions to refer to so that you won't get confused.

If your boss introduces you to a colleague, go back to your desk and write down the person's name. Think of how stressful it would be to forget someone's name, which you are bound to do because you are meeting so many people. If your boss explains the procedure for completing a particular task, write it down. The next time, he or she may ask you to do it on your own.

Taking notes as you learn new things has two benefits. The first, of course, is that it helps you to remember what you've been told. The second benefit comes from your boss's observations. If your boss sees you writing down your tasks, he or she will realize that you've got it going on, that you're on the ball. Your boss won't have to worry whether or not you'll remember everything he or she is telling you afterward. Therefore, taking notes not only keeps you from stressing out over forgetting things, but it will boost your boss's confidence in you, as well.

51.

Reorganize Your Time

Your job comes with many new experiences, people, and skills to learn about. With it also comes the need to organize your time. In some ways, your time is no longer your own. For a certain number of hours each day, you must dedicate your time to your job and career. In the past, you might have had a job, but your time was probably more flexible at that point in your life. Now you have rigid hours devoted specifically to work. This can be a comfort in some ways, and in others it can be a burden, especially if you've become used to a certain schedule.

Reorganizing your time doesn't mean that you have to give things up, though there are some things that you may want to pass up now. It merely means that you have to reshuffle the deck a bit. Depending on your new working hours, you might find yourself unable to tackle the responsibilities you have outside the workplace because of time constraints. You need to restructure your schedule to fit it all in. Think logically about the time you have, and then find a way to get to the post office, the bank, and the grocery store. You might not be able to go first thing in the morning, as you're used to doing, because now you commute and have a bus to catch. Find another time to do these things—maybe you can do some of them on the way home from work or early in the morning on the weekend.

Planning out your time is really a way of organizing your life. Once you figure out how all of the pieces of your puzzle fit together, you'll feel a lot less stressed out.

52.

Explore Your
Work Neighborhood

When you begin a new job, you enter a whole new environment. The office building itself will start to feel like your home away from home, and your cubicle or office space will feel like your room in that home.

Just as you don't stay holed up in your room at home, don't get stuck inside your office, fixated on new tasks and responsibilities. Get out and explore your neighborhood, especially if it's in a different area from where you live. If you're commuting from the suburbs into the city, take the chance to check out the city blocks around your building. If you're driving to an office complex out in the suburbs, get in the car during lunch hour and explore. You may find shops or businesses that catch your interest and take your mind off work for a little while. You may locate some of the best restaurants for takeout lunches or meals with colleagues. You might even discover something useful that could help you with your job.

It's so easy while at work to get caught up in the day-to-day grind. Once your career gets going, it may seem as if nothing can stop you. You're determined, tireless, and fearless. Or perhaps it's the complete opposite. You may find that your new job isn't quite what you had expected. Counting the hours—or the minutes—until you return home is a miserable way to spend the day.

A few minutes outside of the office can help clear your head. Remind yourself that there's more going on in the world than what is happening behind the closed doors of your office. View the neighborhood around your new job as an escape, just as you once viewed the neighborhood that you lived in as a kid. Explore its possibilities, and use them to your best advantage.

53.

Become Absorbed
in Your New Job

In college, you might have felt one of two ways. You might have relished the idea of becoming absorbed in your career, or you might have fought against the notion, vowing that you would never let work become more important to you than your friends or your family.

You're right for feeling this way, of course. However, don't let it start to bother you if you find that you do, after all, enjoy your job. There's nothing wrong with having a good time while you work or feeling good about your job. There's also nothing wrong with feeling proud about the paycheck you earn.

If there's any time in your life to be a workaholic, it's now. For the most part, no one is depending on you. Most likely, no one expects you home at a certain hour. No one expects you take him or her to the park, or to contribute to the household, or just to be there for them. Now you actually have the time to become absorbed in your job—and there's nothing wrong with that!

Okay, so maybe it goes against everything that you felt or believed in college. That's part of the process of moving on. Your feelings will change, and so will your attitudes. It's perfectly normal, and it's perfectly acceptable.

Allow yourself to become absorbed with your job. In a way, it's almost more liberating than *not* being absorbed. Giving yourself over to your job is like letting go. You're not bucking your own system of what you should or shouldn't do. Instead, you're allowing your mind—and your heart—to do what feels normal.

Being absorbed in your job is a good thing. It means not only that you enjoy what you're doing, but that you're giving yourself to it one hundred percent. Remember to recharge, and you can keep on giving for years to come.

54.

Set Aside
Time for Yourself

You love your new job—or perhaps you hate it. Either way, it just might take up more time than you thought. Before you were working, you probably rationalized that most jobs require only forty hours a week.

The problem is that work is a lot more consuming than just forty hours a week. Work really begins as soon as you get up in the morning. Taking a shower, having breakfast, choosing your work outfit, commuting to work—it's all part of your workday. After-work hours are similar. Before you know it, your work week is really more like ninety hours—let's say from six in the morning until nine at night. This doesn't even include any time you decide to work overtime or bring work home.

You're not the only one who has discovered that work takes up much more time than the specified forty hours a week. Try to view others who have always worked a forty-hour work week with a bit more respect. Remember when you couldn't understand why your parents were always so tired at the end of the day? Now you know.

So every week, try to set some time aside for yourself. Even though your job is ultimately for you, the rewards are sometimes not very immediate. It always feels as if you're doing things for someone else—your boss, the company, a client. Although there may be positive rewards for you down the road, right now, you may feel stressed out, overworked, and overlooked.

Do something for yourself. Make it something you enjoy doing. Take time to go to a movie or read a good book. Go out to your favorite restaurant, or take a long, relaxing walk at the beach. You might even just find some quiet time to reflect on things that are important to you—family, friends, or personal spirituality. Don't obsess over what you're going to do, and don't try to squeeze it in to your already burgeoning schedule. Sneak in a guilty pleasure every now and then, just because.

55.

Accept That
You Will Make Mistakes

You've been at your job for a few months. Things are going along rather smoothly. You're confident that you've mastered your responsibilities, and you're happy with your abilities.

Then the day comes when you make a mistake. Time for a reality check!

Mistakes are a fact of life. Everyone makes them, even your boss. No matter how hard you try, no matter how many notes you've taken or how well you think you understand a procedure, one day something will fall through the cracks. It's how you deal with it that's important.

Realize that you will make mistakes. That doesn't mean that you should sit around agonizing about your work, wondering if you have, indeed, made a terrible error. Imagining that small mistakes are disasters is counterproductive.

Instead, listen calmly to your boss as he or she explains what you've done wrong. It's okay to apologize—that's a natural instinct when we do something wrong. But also make sure that you thank your boss for taking the time to explain your mistake. Learn from your mistake, but don't think that it's the end of the world. It isn't!

Mistakes will happen. In most circumstances, your boss is not going to fire you because you made a mistake. Also remember that most mistakes can be fixed. So fix it and forget about it. Accept that you'll probably make mistakes again, but the positive side is that with each mistake, you'll learn something new.

56.

Survive Your
First Company Meeting

Y ou've probably glimpsed it as you walk down the hallway to
the copy room—the conference room with its extra long table
and a dozen or so chairs. You've seen the senior executives in there,
looking serious and studious as they discuss financial reports or
marketing strategies. Part of you wishes that someday you might be
part of upper management, privy to a meeting that will give you
more earth-shattering matters to attend to than sending your boss's
faxes.

However, when the day comes to attend that meeting, you may
find yourself nervous and intimidated. Relax! Without a doubt,
your first company meeting will be scary. You will be surrounded by
the work hierarchy, possibly with a few assistants thrown in. You'll
worry about where you should sit, how you should act, and what
you should say. Those are all perfectly normal issues to think about.
You're not being crazy or overreacting.

At the same time, you need to realize that a company meeting does not take place in a black hole. It has a definite beginning and a definite ending. View the time in between as the great unknown. Try to feel excited about it, rather than stressed. In most cases, your boss will want you to sit in to give you a new perspective on the company. You will probably not be asked to contribute, so don't even worry about it. Do take notes. It shows that you're interested. Your boss will notice, as will other executives. Taking notes also prevents your mind from wandering, which can be embarrassing if you are called on to suggest an idea or voice an opinion. If you have notes written down, you can pretend to scan them while you wait for lightning to strike your brain with an intelligent contribution.

Getting through your first company meeting is merely a matter of survival, mainly because you don't know what to expect. Try not to get too stressed, and it will make the experience much more tolerable—maybe even enjoyable.

57.

Listen with an Open Mind
During Your First Review

Throughout school, you were given performance evaluations—grades on a report card. Sometimes a comment or two might have been written down, but rarely did you meet with your teacher face to face. The equivalent of the report card in the work world is the review. The difference is that you often have to meet with your reviewer—usually your boss—face to face.

Nobody likes to have their faults pointed out. Nobody likes to have someone sit them down and describe all the things they're doing wrong. Your boss will probably be a bit more tactful than that, but it will still sound the same to your ears. No matter how your boss slices it, you're still not perfect.

The easiest way to get through that first review is to keep an open mind. Don't go in expecting to hear about your progress in glowing terms. At the same time, don't go in expecting to hear totally horrible things, either. Whatever you hear, keep your head

126

about you. If your boss offers up some criticisms, don't go on the defense. Don't explain yourself. Don't begin to sweat if the list of things you could improve on seems a whole lot longer than the things you do well. Getting upset won't help. Instead, try to keep in mind what your boss is telling you. Afterward, you may want to think of ways that you might perform better in the areas where your boss thinks you need to improve.

Reviews are important at work. The trick is not to let them overwhelm you. View them as a way to boost your confidence and as a means of keeping track with the pace of your career. Promotions and raises are based on reviews. Learn from your first review, and acknowledge what is said about you. Observations made during a review about what you need to change are almost always things you can work on down the road.

58.

Be Open to
New Experiences

This one might seem like a given. Starting a new job is a new experience. By accepting the new job, you've already shown that you're open to new experiences, right? Experiences in the workplace will definitely be new to you. It's how you approach these new experiences that will help you cope with them.

For example, suppose at college you always worked on an Apple computer. However, your new job requires you to learn how to use a Windows-based system. You refuse to adapt, telling everyone who will listen that Macs are much better computers. Are you demonstrating that you're open to new ideas and experiences? Absolutely not! And you just might be ostracizing yourself in the process.

Here's another example. Suppose you interned at a high-profile advertising agency. Now you've taken on a job with a smaller company. Their ideas and practices are not what you learned at the bigger, more prestigious firm, so you continue to point out the errors of their ways. How do you think your advice will be received? Probably not very well.

Open yourself up to new possibilities, new experiences, and new ways of thinking. Expand your world by keeping an open mind. That's not to say that you should never, ever share something that you've learned. But *sharing* and *telling* are two different things. If you open yourself up to others' ideas, you'll stop struggling against them. Then you won't always feel that you have to debate the merits of your views.

59.

Exchange New Experiences
with Fellow Grads

How do you think you're doing at your new job? How do you feel about your career so far? Is it meeting your expectations? Are you disappointed about some things? Do you still feel confused and unsure about where you want your career to go, or even if you're on the right path to begin with?

The people who will most understand where you're coming from are your fellow college graduates. They probably have the same doubts and concerns as you. Oh, sure, they might not want to admit it at first. Maybe there are even a few out there who are ultimately, supremely happy with their decisions. Good for them!

But no matter where your fellow graduates are emotionally, they are all in the same exact situation as you—a few months out of college, with new experiences to share and new ideas to discuss.

Get together with some recent college grads that you know. They can be old buddies from school, or colleagues your own age at work who have also just graduated. Talk about whether or not your jobs were all you thought they would be. What are you disappointed about? What did you find pleasantly surprising? How are you adapting to life in the "real" world?

As you listen to your friends recount their own after-college experiences, you'll realize new things about yourself, too. You'll be able to compare how you feel about life so far with the feelings of your friends. You'll come to realize that you're not the only one who might find work a lot more absorbing than you thought it would be. As you do so, you'll reinforce your own positive experiences, while being able to laugh about and minimize the negative ones.

60.

Compartmentalize
Responsibilities at Work

Sometimes there just might be times when you don't want to get out of bed and face another day of work. You lie there, with all of your responsibilities looming before you. Some may still be mundane, boring, and time-consuming, but they still need to get done. Others may be more challenging, but with the challenges come doubts. As you lie there stressing about all of these things, the tasks you have to handle suddenly seem insurmountable.

Take a deep breath. You need to reevaluate your workload, and one of the best ways to do that is by compartmentalizing.

When you compartmentalize, the basic idea is to mentally put each task, or a small group of tasks, in its own little "box" or "compartment." For example, suppose you have several tasks that require you to visit the copy room and areas near it. In your mind, put all of those tasks in a "compartment," and get them done together: Make copies, send a fax, drop packages off at the mailroom, and pick up supplies all at once. Suddenly, what was actually four tasks has been knocked down to one.

Suppose your boss is going to a conference and leaving you in charge while he or she is away. The least stressful way to make sure everything gets done on time and in the proper manner is to group your tasks—to compartmentalize. In this way, you won't have to wonder if something didn't get done—you'll *know* it got done. Compartmentalizing allows you to concentrate on several simple tasks at once, giving your brain the freedom to stretch itself for more demanding tasks without cluttering it up.

Learn to compartmentalize. Remember—part of the word "compartmentalize" is "mental." Organize your tasks mentally, and you'll help get rid of the stress.

61.

Extend a Hand to a Colleague

Picture this scenario: You're totally swamped with work. Even though you've compartmentalized, all of the stuff on your to-do list seems to have flooded to tidal wave proportions. Suddenly, a colleague urgently asks for help. What do you do? Do you hide your head and go about your business, or do you lend a hand?

If you feel that there is absolutely no way for you to help out without compromising your own work, then by all means, don't add to your own stress level. But if by some chance, you feel that you can spare some time, extend that hand to your colleague in need. There is much to be gained by helping out in a crisis situation.

First of all, your colleague will probably feel indebted to you. It's never a bad thing to have allies in the office, and aiding a fellow worker in the trenches is a sure way to secure one.

Second, taking on work other than your own expands your information base. Think of what you can learn just because you decided to be a nice guy.

Third, it always feels good to do something for someone else. Of course, you may argue that you do stuff for other people all day long. True—but these are the people you work for all the time. These are the people you are expected to help out. Offering your time to someone you normally don't work with shows that you're a team player. For just a few moments, it also takes some time away from your own troubles. In fact, you might realize that your work is more interesting than you thought when you see what other people have to do around the office!

Lending a hand shows everyone that you're willing to pitch in and go the extra mile when needed. If you have the time, help out. You never know when that could come back to benefit you.

62.

Accept Learning
Opportunities Gladly

Your boss has asked you to attend a special seminar to learn a new technique in your field. You're the only one in your department who was invited to go. Upon returning, your boss would like you to fill in the rest of the group on what you learned. How do you react?

Or how about this: Your boss has given you a new project to tackle. Along with more responsibilities come new things to learn and new procedures to memorize. No one else is asked to do these things. No one else has to do his or her own job, along with learning and taking on more work.

In both scenarios, say thank you—and mean it! Obviously, you're doing something right. Your boss has selected you for these challenges. You should do your best to prove to your boss that he or she made the correct choice.

Accept new learning opportunities gladly. Instead of letting your mind get mired in all of the added responsibilities and pressures, get excited about the possibilities. Remind yourself that this is one of the reasons why you are working—to learn more so that you can move up to the job you really want.

Accept new opportunities with gratitude. Don't view them as additional stress factors, but as rewards for doing well at your job. And don't forget to congratulate yourself. Your boss chose *you*. Good job!

63.

Find a Mentor

As a child and young adult, you had parents or family members to guide you. In college, you had professors and guidance counselors to point you in the right direction. These people took an interest in you and tried to teach you what they'd learned from their own experiences.

Now more than ever, you could again benefit from someone like that—a mentor. A mentor is that special person who has decided to take you under his or her wing. A mentor is much more than just a boss. A mentor is someone who recognizes your potential; someone who goes out of their way to point out things you can improve; someone who helps you hone your skills and develop new ones.

You might not recognize your mentor right away—and you certainly can't go up to someone and ask them to be your mentor. Instead, look for someone whom you admire where you work. This can be your boss, or perhaps someone else in your department a little bit further along than you in his or her career. Take note of anyone with whom you are comfortable that shows an interest in the projects you are working on and asks how you like the job. Share something with this person that you are currently working on. Ask for his or her advice. Encourage this person to share insights and suggestions. There is a chance that you will develop a meaningful friendship with this person, and he or she may be invaluable to you, both as a colleague and as a friend, as you work your way up from your entry-level position.

Navigating your way through a professional environment can be hard. A mentor can help you learn more quickly, point out mistakes to watch for, and alert you to possible pitfalls. People love sharing wisdom that they've learned from experience. Finding someone to help you along, to serve as an example, is one way to avoid getting sidetracked by the everyday stresses of work.

64.

Ignore Office Gossip

It's so easy to get caught up in it. "Did you hear what so-and-so did?" "Really? Well, I heard that so-and-so did blah-blah-blah." Gossip of any sort always seems like fun. Not only is it a way to bond with your fellow workers, but it's also entertaining. It can be a stress-reliever to talk about problems other than your own.

Gossip of any kind, however, quickly loses its shine when rumors abound and the things that are said end up hurting people. Office gossip can be especially damaging. It can not only hurt someone's feelings, but their professional life. A hard-won reputation can easily be forgotten when someone becomes the topic of conversation around the water cooler.

Avoid gossip before it even gets started. Gossip is destructive, yet it seems to be in our nature to listen to it. On some level, it makes us feel better about ourselves. We usually only gossip when someone does something foolish. Laughing about someone else's mishaps makes our own mistakes seem less embarrassing. This kind of treatment is cruel and unfair to whomever is the subject of the gossip.

Gathering around the coffee machine to talk about the latest TV show or football game is fine, but once the conversation starts turning catty, take the high road and leave. Don't be snooty about it—after all, you don't want to be fodder for the gossip mill. Just politely excuse yourself, claiming you have things to do.

If all else fails, imagine how you would feel if you overheard or learned that people were gossiping about you. Depending on the subject, you might feel totally crushed. Don't foist those feelings on someone else. You'll only end up in a situation where you or someone you work with gets hurt.

65.

Don't Burn Bridges

It is often hard to mix personal and professional lives. You want to like all of the people that you work with, and you want them to like you, but the world doesn't always work that way. To think that you will never come up against a difficult professional relationship is idealistic. It's inevitable. You won't get along with everyone. Some people at work may become your best friends. Some you may only be able to tolerate. And then there will be those select few whom you would like to see leave the office and never return.

The best thing you can do is not let negative relationships get to you. Don't ignore people that you are having trouble with. Remain professional. Do the best job that you can when working with them. Don't cater to them, but work with them, not against them. It could make all the difference down the road.

One of the biggest lessons to learn in the working world is never to burn bridges with anyone. Your difficult coworker could someday end up being the CEO of the new company you eventually go to work for. It's best that people remember you as maintaining a professional manner at all times. Many fields have a very narrow scope. You begin to understand how small the professional community is when people you worked with in the past show up in other companies.

Networking all begins with that first job right out of college. Unless you plan on switching careers midstride, you need all of the allies you can get. And because they will probably move on at some point, too, someone might just be in a position to offer you a bridge over to that dream job that you always wanted.

Don't burn bridges. It will be one less thing to worry about, and one more thing that will help you in the end.

66.

Congratulate Colleagues
Who Get Promoted

Here's a tough one to swallow. You and a few other college grads were hired at about the same time. You both entered with the same degrees, the same amount of education under your belts, and all other things basically equal. You don't all work for the same boss, but you do the same type of job.

One day a memo lands in your mailbox. One of your fellow college grads has been promoted. Even if it hurts you, try to congratulate your office mate. It may be difficult to absorb. You're bound to feel jealous, as well as discouraged and insecure.

Understand that your time will come. View your colleague's promotion as something that has come to you all, as a group. After all, if your company is willing to promote your coworker, then it will probably promote the rest of you, too.

Promotions in a career are steps along the success ladder. Looking forward to promotions is what gives the daily grind purpose.

It's what makes your job seem worthwhile. Be happy for your colleague—and mean it. All of the things that come along with the promotion—business cards, new office space, a job title—these are all small things. Consider your own job satisfaction and your own goals. Sometime soon, you will probably get promoted, too.

67.

Volunteer for
New Responsibilities

One way to show others that you're serious about your job, that you want to move ahead in your career, is to volunteer for new responsibilities. Although volunteering to tackle something new definitely helps your boss, it also benefits you. It alerts your boss to the fact that you're ready to move on. It lets your boss know that you're anxious to learn more, if there's more work to go around (and usually there is). It saves your boss the trouble of having to ask you if you're ready for new challenges, ultimately saving him or her time.

Volunteering for more responsibility will ultimately advance your career. Taking the initiative to ask for more will show your boss that you are capable of more. You are willing to take on more work, and to come to the aid of your colleagues. It demonstrates your interest and enthusiasm, which will only help in the end.

68.

Forget Stupid Things That
You Think You Said

Maybe you're the type of person who openly expresses your feelings. You have no trouble telling others how you feel, relaying your ideas on work-related topics, and giving your opinion when someone asks. Or maybe you're the type of person who is shy around the office. You think through everything you say before you say it, hoping that you don't sound like an idiot and say the wrong thing.

But it will happen. One day, you'll open your mouth, and whether you intend to or not, you'll hear yourself say something completely ridiculous. You'll go back to your desk and berate yourself. You'll play the conversation over and over again in your head, wondering where it went wrong and how you could have avoided it.

You need to stop right there. First of all, you're probably blowing out of proportion what you *think* you said. We have a tendency to

147

see our mistakes as gigantic catastrophes. Imagine if someone else had said what you did. Does it sound all that bad now?

Others probably did not perceive what you said as stupid. Even though you may feel that you really stuck your foot in your mouth, it's probably not as bad as you imagine. Most likely, no one even noticed.

Forget about it. Not everybody says the right thing all the time. Accept that you *might* have said something foolish, and move on.

69.

Don't Be Put Off by
Real-World Responsibilities

When people mention the "real" world, they're talking about "grownup" responsibilities. They're talking about getting away from the security blanket of your family and college and standing on your own two feet—in the "real" world.

You've probably taken on many real-world responsibilities already without even realizing it. Your job is part of this real world. So are any bills you pay on your own. You might even already understand how difficult it is to juggle a paycheck and your bills.

Real-world responsibilities are part of life. There is pressure in managing your career and your finances, but part of graduating college is learning how to make mature decisions. The choice between buying a new jacket and paying the electric bill puts your maturity level to the test. Do you do the responsible thing, or do you do what you think would be fun?

This is not to say that the real world can't be fun, either. Anything is fun, within the parameters you set. College wasn't always entertaining. The reality of college was exams and term papers—but probably, the overall view you have of it is that it was a lot of fun.

Accept the new responsibilities of the real world as the reward for graduating. You are fortunate to be standing on your own!

70.

Take Your Time
Making Life Decisions

If life immediately after college is frustrating you, take a deep breath. You're not alone. You graduated with such high hopes. Maybe those hopes have been realized and everything is going along smoothly. Or maybe you think that you made some really colossal errors in judgment, and the only way to rectify them is to make a complete and total change.

Take the time to consider if change is really the answer. Sometimes it is. But sometimes the change you're looking for only brings about more stress.

It is important to remember to take your time making life decisions. Don't jump into anything too hastily, especially if you're doing it out of frustration or on a whim. It's quite possible that the changes you bring about will be irreversible, and you could be in a worse position than when you started.

That's not to say that you should never make changes. Change, of course, is good. That's what graduating from college is all about—change. Yet at the same time, any changes you make should be thought through carefully. Sit with your idea and reflect upon it. Make sure it's exactly what you want. The new opportunity you're probably looking for isn't going anywhere. Just be certain that you're making the change for the right reasons, and you'll be happier and more secure in your decision.

71.

Move Out,
On, and Up

At some point after graduation, you're going to have cut the cord. It may be the one that connects you to your family, or even the one that connects you to your college friends. Either way, the time will come when you'll need to move out, move on, and move up. Now that you're out of college, you may expect to be more independent, and that probably calls for getting your very own place to live. It's not going to be as painful as you think. In fact, you're probably even ready for it.

Moving out—whether it is from your parents' home or your friends' group house—is indeed a scary proposition. But it's also a lot of fun. Think about it! The remote control is yours! The friends you invite over are yours! Everything in the refrigerator is yours!

The time will come when it just feels right to you. You will be willing to take on all of the good and bad parts of being on your own. Make the move! Truly step out on your own! The only way is up.

72.

Accumulate in Steps

Don't expect that as soon as you step out on your own, your life will fall magically into place. Your career might be stable, but it's not your dream job yet. Your apartment might be in a great neighborhood, but you have no furniture yet. You have a few more pieces for your portfolio, but not quite enough yet. You've been dating around a bit, but you haven't met anyone special—yet.

The word "yet" may only be three letters, but it can be very powerful, loaded with possibilities. It implies that things are yet to come, that even though you may have moved on, you still have a way to go. You may not have a long way, but you're still traveling.

And that's just fine. Don't expect everything to fall into place at once. If that were to happen, it might be too much too soon. Take things leisurely and slowly, step by step.

For example, so what if you don't have all the furniture for your apartment? Buy it piece by piece. Compare your house to your career. In your career, you didn't jump straight from college into the

CEO position. You have to accumulate the skills, the promotions, and the know-how. You haven't gotten there yet, but you will. It's all a matter of putting it together, piece by piece.

Concentrate on what you're able to accumulate or do now. Don't stress yourself out by looking at the whole picture. View it in individual pieces. Once you finish one section, you can move on to the next. Once you buy your dining room table, you can start saving for the chairs.

73.

Set Up a Budget

As a college student, you had a few things that you absolutely had to spend money on. Perhaps you had tuition fees, books, and rent. Even when you started your job, you probably still had a few financial obligations, but nothing to sweat over. You were either splitting the cost with roommates or contributing at home to your family.

Now things are different. Now the financial burden is all yours. That's a lot of pressure. But it doesn't have to be if you analyze your finances and realize that there is enough money to go around.

This is in no way meant to be a guide to financial planning, but a few simple steps will help you beat the "I don't have any money" blues. It can all be summed up in one word: "budget."

Write down how much income you receive per year after taxes and insurance deductions, and divide by twelve. This is how much money you have to spend each month. Then add up what you estimate your bills will be. Include everything: rent, utilities, phone, cable, commuting costs, car and renter's insurance, gas, college-loan payments, pet food—whatever you know you have to spend money on. Then subtract this figure from your monthly paycheck total, and *voila!* This is how much money is left over.

Don't get depressed if it's not as much as you hoped. What you need to do now is divide that number by four, for approximately four weeks in each month. This is how much money you can spend every week. This is what you have left over to buy groceries and any other essentials you need. This is the money you have to spend with friends or treat coworkers at happy hour. This, basically, is your budget.

The trick is to try not to spend more than your budget will allow. Once you do, and you can't pay your bills, it's hard to brush financial pressures off as nothing to worry about. That's why you should take care of them now. Paying bills is part of the real world. Write those checks, and mail them out. You'll find the real world much easier to handle.

74.

Save a Little Money
Each Week

It sounds impossible, doesn't it? You've just been told that you have to stick to a budget, that you have to pay your bills, that you shouldn't fall behind, that this will lead to a stress-free environment. Well, so will putting aside a little money for yourself every week.

Your paycheck is your reward for working. Every week, you spend forty-plus hours at your job, and the payoff is the paycheck. Most of it goes to keeping your life running. You begin to think that the only purpose in life is to work, to earn a paycheck, and to spend it on bills again, which means you have to keep working to earn more money, because the bills never end.

That's why you need to put a little money aside for yourself. It doesn't have to be a lot of money. Start off with ten dollars a week. After a year, that's $520. It might not sound like a lot in the grand scheme of things, but it's more than you had when you started. If ten dollars feels comfortable, then double it. Then you'll have over a thousand dollars after a year.

What you choose to do with your money is up to you. A financial planner would tell you to invest it, to start saving now for your retirement. That's great advice. But perhaps you'd rather spend your hard-earned money on something else, like a new sofa, or a down payment on a car, or even—after you've saved enough—a Caribbean vacation. The key word here is that it's *your* hard-earned money. Pay the bills you have to pay, and then try to put something in the bank. It could be the best money that you *don't* spend.

75.

Don't Spend Money on
Things That You Don't Really Need

Sometimes you can get so caught up in living on your own that you end up buying a whole lot of stuff that you don't really need. Being on your own gives you a wonderful sense of freedom. But with that freedom, like everything else outside of college, comes responsibility. Spending money on things that you really don't need rather than paying the bills—or even saving your money—is not very responsible.

It's so tempting, though! You've waited for this chance your whole life—to have your own money and buy what you want, when you want it. No one else is around to tell you not to spend your money on this or that. However, think back on that advice before you make your purchases.

Curb your desire to buy a lot of silly things that are unnecessary right now. Keeping your bank account balanced takes self-control.

Weigh what will happen if you buy that spiffy, flat-screen TV with what will happen if you can't meet your rent payment. That flat-screen TV will look nice—but only if you have an apartment to put it in.

76.

Experiment If Your Job
Takes an Unexpected Turn

Sometimes your job may throw you a curve ball. You're coasting along, thinking you've got it all under control. You know where you're headed, you're confident that you've made the right decisions, and you're secure in everything that you're doing on the job.

Then suddenly—wham! Your job sends you a blow that totally shakes you up. This unexpected turn could be anything. It could be your boss switching to another company and wanting to take you along. It could be a shift in responsibilities from one department to another, which takes away some projects you have but gives you new ones. Perhaps you get a job offer from a friend of a friend of a friend in an area you've never considered. Maybe you're the casualty of that dreaded word—*downsizing*.

If something unexpected happens, explore your options. Try not to go through the "woe is me" syndrome, where you shake your head with discouragement, believing that only negative things

happen to you. Make this unexpected turn into s[...]
Experiment in an area that never occurred to yo[...]
with your boss if he or she asks. Try something n[...]
responsibilities shift.

Right now, you're learning and discovering n[...]
your career. Experimenting is the perfect way [...]
discoveries. So what do you do if your job throws y[...]
Make the most of it. In most cases, you'll end up ah[...]

th[...]
th[...]
is[...]

y[...]
c[...]
t[...]
c[...]

77.

You're Not Doing It the
Hard Way—Just Your Way

It's funny how everyone always seems to know what's best for you. No one can believe you might be following the path that you have thought about and consciously chosen. The perfect answer for all of these people who want you to do things their way, because their way is obviously better, is to tell them that you're doing it *your* way.

Don't argue with your friends, family, or significant other about your choices. Don't defend yourself. This will only make your loved ones come at you full force. If you truly believe that you're doing things the best way that you know how—and that includes things in your job, at your home, and in your relationship with your boyfriend or girlfriend—then you'll be secure enough not to state your case.

However, if what people say starts to bother you, just remind yourself that you're not doing it their way, or the hard way. You're doing it *your* way. You're following what you believe to be the

proper path to take. You're following your heart where a love interest is concerned. You're handling your responsibilities to the best of your abilities. To them it might look like the hard way. Thank them for their advice and their concern—and remember that you're doing things the way that you want to do them.

78.

Ignore Negative Comments
from Friends and Family

Oftentimes, when we choose to ignore criticism that comes our way from family and friends, their comments begin to escalate. Instead of urging you to take their advice, those around you may actually begin to categorize the decisions you've made as bad ones. In many cases, well-meaning loved ones may tell you that you have made wrong decisions and are risking your future success.

What should you do? Should you take the bait? Should you get in a shouting match? Will that solve anything?

Of course not. Not everyone is going to agree with the things that you do. Even though you're out on your own, paying for yourself, and working a steady job, family and friends still might see you the way that they know you. Your family still may see you as the kid who accidentally set the hedges on fire. Your friends still may see you as the person who nabbed the sign off the dean's office door. They expect you to do silly things. They're used to pointing out the errors of your ways, perhaps even if there are no longer any errors being made.

Ignore those negative comments. Don't give in to the need to fight back and defend yourself. You'll never convince them that they're wrong, and you may say things that you'll later regret. Tension between friends or family and you is something you definitely don't need.

In the same vein, try not to be negative to your friends or any family members that are around your own age. Encourage them, and be positive and supportive about their choices. Realize that just as you may ignore negative comments that your friends dish out, they'll probably do the same. Keep doing what you're doing, and do it the best that you can. Your friends and family will come around, although it may take some time.

79.

Don't Worry If
You Don't Like Your First Job

Here's a news flash—in all likelihood, your first job will not be your last job or your only job. So if you're not too thrilled with it and it's not all you had hoped it would be, don't worry. You won't be at this job forever.

Of course, you *want* to like your job. You probably had high expectations for your first real taste of a position in your chosen field. In some ways, you've waited your whole life for this opportunity. Now, as you sit at your desk or work on an assignment that you really don't like, you can only wonder what you were thinking.

What you were thinking was about the big picture. And that's what you have to keep in mind right now. No matter how disenchanted you become with your first job, it's just a glimpse of the whole picture of your career.

So don't despair if your first job isn't all that you hoped it would be. It's a stepping stone, a milepost. Eventually, you will move on.

80.

Weigh the Paycheck
with Job Satisfaction

Ah! This is where all those ideals you used to shout about in college come in: "I don't need a lot of money to make me happy! As long as my job is satisfying, that's all the reward I need!"

It's a wonderful sentiment, but sometimes it doesn't apply to the "real" world. After all, if you're now on your own, you have bills to pay. Your paycheck goes for something more than just spending it with your friends on the weekend. Your paycheck has meaning in the "real" world.

Well, so does job satisfaction. Nothing is more stressful than going to work each day and absolutely dreading it. Your lofty goal of working not for money but for pleasure is partially a good aspiration. It's very important to enjoy what you do. Along with the paycheck, enjoying your job makes working worthwhile.

So what happens if you feel that you'd be happier at a job that is more enjoyable to you but has a lower salary? What should you do?

You need to weigh what's important to you. This might mean that you have to downsize your life if you choose to take a lesser-paying job. You might have to give up your apartment and move back in with friends. Which is more important—your lifestyle or job satisfaction? Also, you might be taking a step away from your career goals. Are you really happy at your current job, or will this new opportunity be more satisfying to you?

There is no correct answer. Friends and family can offer advice, but only you can make the decision that's right for you. Think about what will make you happiest—whether it's the paycheck or the more satisfying job. In time, you'll probably be able to combine the two.

81.

Factor in Your Interests
and Your Lifestyle

One way to keep your job satisfying and to make sure that it doesn't take over your life is to factor in your interests and lifestyle. For example, suppose you've always been partial to the country. You like open spaces, being outdoors on the weekends, and knowing the people in the community you are living in. The company that hired you, however, is in the city.

You decide to try something new and move to the city, but it's just not working out. It's not making you happy. Perhaps it's the city environment, with the added pressures of a lot of people and taking public transportation rather than simply jumping in your car. If your lifestyle isn't making you happy, then chances are that your job will suffer in the process.

Instead of working, you find yourself gazing out the window, wishing that you were somewhere else. In this case, your true, heartfelt interests are getting in the way of your job satisfaction. It could be time for a change. Review your options. See if there's a way to bring a little bit of your lifestyle or interests into your current work environment. If that's not possible, then it might be time to move on. Nothing's worse than dreading the workday ahead of you. If you can't balance it with a lifestyle that you like and interests that make you happy—if the job is too confining, restrictive, or all-consuming—then the time might be right to consider other opportunities.

If you honestly gave it your best shot, then realize that you need more to keep you happy, that's okay. Now plan a change and look forward to it. The change to come will be the light at the end of your workday tunnel.

82.

Don't Try to Answer
the Relationship Question

The dating game. On top of everything else you have going on—the job, the apartment, the bills, high expectations—you might have someone special in your life. Perhaps this person alleviates some of your pressures. Or perhaps having this person in your life adds to your current pressures.

It's not always the specific person, or even the relationship that causes pressure. It's the questions that plague you, not only from yourself, but from family and friends. Others constantly inquire about the status of your relationship and where it may be going.

Try not to let other people's views on relationships sway your own. Don't feel pressured to turn a pleasant dating experience into a lifelong commitment just because people hint that you're the "right" age. First of all, people do tend to get married later in life now than they once did. Putting off the marriage decision for a few years is perfectly acceptable. Second, you'll know when it's right.

You'll know when you feel you can commit to one and only one person.

Marriage *is* a big deal, but worrying about it doesn't need to be, especially now. When others badger you about it, tell them that you're simply not ready to answer that question yet, much less "pop the question."

83.
Complain Less and Enjoy More

Life can be very difficult, especially when you are in a period of transition. Pressures mount, and it's very easy to complain. In fact, sometimes it seems easier to dwell on the negatives than to enjoy the positives. We expect life to be happy. Lately, though, it may feel as if it's been one big chore.

Don't let complaining become the norm. It's very easy to sit around with your colleagues during lunch and complain about your boss, or about company policy, or about why someone got promoted when you didn't. In some ways, you may even feel that you're releasing some pent-up angst. By getting your complaints off your chest, you feel a bit better. In reality, however, complaining serves no purpose. It doesn't solve problems. It doesn't improve your situation. It leaves you and those around you with a bad taste of what your life is like.

Try to focus instead on the good things. Think about what you really like about your job, your apartment, or even the person you are dating. Instead of finding faults, enjoy the positives.

That's the bottom line. If you're looking to complain and find fault, then you will. Of course, there are going to be times when your complaints are legitimate. But if you find that you're complaining just for the sake of complaining, try to concentrate on the things that you enjoy instead.

84.

Don't Compare
Your Progress with Others'

Viewing your colleagues as competitors can lead to anxiety and pettiness, a combination that can only bring failure. Focusing in on who has a bigger office, who makes more money, and who was invited to a meeting will quickly land you nowhere. It is the fastest road to unemployment, or at the very least, complete job dissatisfaction.

Don't compare yourself and your progress at work with that of others in your company, or even with that of your friends. So your best friend is moving along faster than you are at her company. Big deal! So another guy at work was asked to accompany his boss on a conference to Los Angeles. So what? None of this has anything to do with you.

It's hard not to compare ourselves with others. We do it all the time. We're always holding ourselves up to some higher ideal, inspecting ourselves against standards set by others.

Try not to. So many variables go into having a successful career, and not all of them are in your control. Concentrate on your progress, and yours alone, and don't obsess over the fact that the colleague you worked with in marketing was just asked to take on a major account.

Be careful what you wish for. Just think of all the new pressures he now has to deal with!

85.

If You Can't Have a Dog, Get a Cat

Wanting something that doesn't fit your lifestyle can add dissatisfaction and pressure to your life. Learn about compromise. To satisfy that urge, perhaps something slightly different will satisfy you just as well.

Maybe you are dying to get a dog—but when you actually think about it, there is no way that you can take care of one. What will happen if you have to work late? Who will let the dog out? Can you really afford to take care of all the dog's needs? Besides, in some cities, it's not easy to find places for rent that will let you have a dog. Obviously, a dog is not the best choice for you.

A cat, on the other hand, is less demanding, and more landlords will accept cats in spaces they have for rent. A cat doesn't need to be let out or require so much of your attention—though, of course, you have to feed it and make arrangements for care if you go away. The cat can still keep you company; it can still offer the companionship you are seeking from having a pet.

There's the compromise. You've accepted something into your life that's close to what you want, but that fits in more with your lifestyle. At this point in your life (and almost every other time), the need to compromise will come up over and over again. Just keep it simple. Keep the dream, of course, but for now, give the cat a cuddle and enjoy what your lifestyle will accommodate.

86.

Don't Give In to Frustration

Sometimes things just don't work out the way that we planned. No matter how many times we try to fit the pieces together, something just doesn't work. We jam the pieces together, thinking it's got to work out, but it still doesn't.

Try not to give in to frustration. It's very easy to let the tension and pressure build, until one day, you feel like blowing up. It's important to remember that everything passes. If you are having a bad week, and it seems as if you can't take one more curve ball, keep your eye on next week. Seeing the light at the end of the tunnel can help you maintain your equilibrium. After all, you can't "lose it" at work. There is no sense in sacrificing your professionalism. Be careful not to take your frustrations out on friends and family, as well.

Everyone experiences a buildup of tension and frustration. It's a busy world and it seems, at times, that our lives run at a frantic pace. Taking time out to reassess your frustration and put it in perspective can only help diffuse it.

If all else fails, laugh. There is nothing like laughter to help you understand that these are *only* small problems. Don't worry so much about them—they will keep coming. Taking them in stride is what conquering your frustration is all about.

87.

Downtime Is Good Time

In college, you probably had lots of downtime—those moments when your time was your own, when you could hang out with friends or just be by yourself. It wasn't laziness that you enjoyed, but a time to recharge your batteries.

The problem now is that although you can find downtime, you feel guilty when you take it. You are constantly reminding yourself that you should be working. You should go in the office on a Saturday, work late during the week, or take work home, at the very least.

But now, more than ever, with all of the changes that your life is going through, you do need downtime. You need quiet moments to do absolutely nothing. Even your computer needs downtime—it shuts itself off when you're not using it! Don't feel guilty because you rent a favorite movie and decide to stay home instead of going out with your friends. Socializing isn't necessarily downtime. A quiet evening to yourself is.

Downtime is good time. Don't feel you have to fill every minute of every day with important, necessary tasks. Enjoy your downtime. You probably don't have much as it is!

88.

Feel Free to
Change Your Mind

It is said that changing one's mind is a woman's prerogative. In reality, it is everyone's prerogative.

Giving yourself the option of changing your mind takes a tremendous weight off your shoulders. For one thing, feeling that you have no choices, that you have made a decision about your career or your job that is irreversible, is a tremendous strain. Thoughts like, "What have I done?" "What was I thinking?" and "How could I have been so wrong?" crowd your mind. It's like your brain has decided to have a negative field day, and you continually chastise yourself for your error in judgment.

Allow freedom of choice to participate in your brain's field day. Invite a host of other possibilities to join the party. You're not happy in your profession? Change your mind, and choose a new one. You're not happy with your apartment? Change your mind when your lease is up, and move. You're not happy taking a year off between college and work? Change your mind, and start looking for a job now.

You probably changed your mind in college all the time. You might even have changed your mind about your degree. If it was okay then, it's okay now. Don't feel that because you made a decision, you have to stick with it. Of course, you should give it a chance. But if you really don't see any future for yourself in the career that you've chosen, give yourself the option of changing it.

Don't view yourself as someone who can't figure it out or can't make a commitment to a decision. Instead, think of yourself as someone who likes to try different things. You're gazing at the menu, and so much is being offered. So you made what you thought was the right choice. If you don't like how it tastes, feel comfortable sending it back, and choose again.

89.

Reevaluate Your Goals

Once you've been away from college for a while, it's probably a good idea to reevaluate your goals. If you're feeling pressure in your life right now, it could be that you're trying to live up to or maintain goals that no longer apply to your current lifestyle or the choices that you've made. The best thing to do is reevaluate where you are and where you want to be.

If you made a list of goals just before or after graduating, pull them out. Review and truly consider them. Do you still feel the same passion for these goals that you did several months ago? Have your priorities shifted a bit, forcing you to juggle your goals? Have you felt yourself clinging to a long-held belief, only to realize that it no longer matters in your life?

Then reevaluate. Now that you've had a chance to experience your career, consider if the goal that you've set for yourself is the right one. Now that you've been out in the "real" world for a short time, think about whether a lifestyle goal—like owning a house on the water—is still something you truly desire.

You're very aware that things change. Friends change, your life changes, and your job changes. You've changed, too. Graduating from college is a growth process. You're accumulating new experiences and meeting new people. Remember how your goals and thoughts were formulated or changed while you were in college? Well, guess what? They never really stop changing. And neither do you.

That's why it helps to sit down and take stock of those goals. Are they still important to you today, after all that you've been doing? The pressure you've placed upon yourself could be because you have changed and your attitudes have changed, but your goals have not.

Reevaluate your goals. Update them if necessary. Make sure they still have a place in your life.

90.

Trying New Careers
Is Like Trying on New Shoes

Sometimes the possibilities seem overwhelming. There's so much to choose from; so many different options and opportunities. How will you ever be able to choose the right job for you?

If you're still confused about which way to turn in life, perhaps you need to change your outlook a bit. Think of your life and job prospects as shoes in a store. Upon walking in, you see a ton of shoe styles you like. All of them look good. But how will they feel once you try them on? So you start putting them on your feet, looking at them in the mirror. Little by little, you narrow down your choices, until finally you find the style that fits and feels good.

Choosing a job is similar. After a lot of research, speculation, and interviews, you finally select the job that you think is the perfect fit, and everything goes along fine. Until one day, you spot a new shoe in the window. Suddenly you consider buying a new pair. You're about due for a change anyway, aren't you?

Shoes wear out, and jobs start to feel old. What you need to do is find something to make it exciting again. That might mean switching to a new company or taking on new responsibilities. Perhaps you should transfer within your current firm.

If the shoe doesn't fit, then try on another. If your job or company doesn't seem like the perfect fit for you anymore, think about trading in your old shoes for something new.

Slip on those high-tops and take a leap if you need to. Break in a new pair of shoes. Like Cinderella, eventually you will find the perfect fit.

91.

Consider Making a
"Down" Move

Nothing in your life is set in stone. Perhaps you mapped out the proper course you thought that you needed to follow to achieve your goals and make your dream job a reality. You don't want to make any detours, but the scenery beyond your chosen path certainly looks inviting. The only problem is that you've invested a lot of time in your current situation. To get off the road now means you'll have to backtrack.

What happens if an opportunity arises for you to do something else that sounds appealing? It could be in a related field, or perhaps something that you've never even considered. You may have to start at the bottom again. After all, you have no experience in that field. Do you really want to do that?

The answer doesn't lie so much in why you *should* do it, but why you *shouldn't* do it. You know the pros of taking a new job that sounds interesting. You also know the cons: a lower salary, entry-

190

level work, and time you'll have to invest to reeducate yourself. What's the worst thing that could happen if you make a downward move, as long as your current living situation can afford it? If the job doesn't work out, at least you've gained some varied experience. Then you can always get back on the road you were originally on and continue your journey.

Sometimes getting off the road is the best decision you can make, especially if your heart is pulling you in a new direction. It might seem a little foolish as you do it. Friends and family may even ask you to have your head examined. But once you step into that new job and it feels right, you'll know that you made the right choice.

Wondering "what if?" can leave you feeling anxious and unfulfilled. Don't let your doubts plague you. Going "downward" is sometimes the best way to move up.

92.

You Will Find Your Career Niche

There's nothing more depressing than listening to someone go on about the perfect career and job they have, especially if you feel that you still haven't found your niche. You may have a friend or colleague who constantly regales you with stories about the wonderful challenges he or she faces every day, and how the job is everything that he or she hoped it would be.

It's inevitable that you will end up feeling a sense of dissatisfaction. You may be desperate to find your niche—the place where you fit, and a position that brings you a sense of challenge and fulfillment.

Sometimes you may feel as if you keep coming up against a brick wall. You've tried different jobs, you've accepted different responsibilities, you've opened yourself up to change, but still nothing feels right.

Finding your career niche may take longer than you expect. You were probably comfortable with your niche in school. You may have even been comfortable with your entry-level position. But now you want a position to which you feel that you belong.

Don't look too hard for it. Sometimes when you look too hard for something, you miss it completely. One day, you'll be sitting at your desk or working out in the field, and it will hit you—this is it. You've found your niche, and you didn't even realize it!

Take comfort in the fact that you will find your place eventually. You may have to log some long hours, or even make a change, but you will find your niche—if your niche doesn't find you first.

93.

Lend a Hand to
a Friend in Need

Often when we proceed headlong into our careers, we lose sight of everything around us. We put blinders on so that nothing can distract us, and we focus all of our attention on what's directly in front of us. We rationalize that this is what we need to do to get ahead, to succeed. But this attitude can cost us in other areas of our lives. Personal relationships may suffer. Our own mental or physical health can deteriorate.

It would do us some good to remove the blinders every once in a while and remind ourselves of what else is going on out there. One way to do so is to lend a hand to a friend who needs it.

Lending a hand to a friend can take many forms. Perhaps a friend who is a few years younger is getting ready to make the leap from college into the job market. Ask your friend if he would like some help. Or perhaps a friend is getting ready to move, and doesn't want to bother you. After all, you've been so immersed in your job that she barely sees you anymore. Offer up your services. Or maybe your friend just needs someone to listen, as you needed him or her to listen a few months back. Lend an ear, instead of a hand. That takes hardly any effort at all.

The daily pressures of a new job and a new life can make you lose perspective. Your focus becomes all about you. And thinking about oneself all of the time can be draining! Take off the blinders. Focus in again on the people around you, and lend someone who may need it your help or support.

94.
Expect to Feel Tired
After Work

You think that there's something wrong with you. After a long day at work, all you want to do is sit in front of the TV, eat a pizza, and then fall asleep. You've never felt so tired. It doesn't make sense. You used to be out until dawn in school, and then get up for an eight o'clock class. You used to tend bar till two in the morning, and still have enough energy to hit the all-night diner.

What's happened to you? Why don't you want to go out after work and socialize with your office buddies? Or meet up with old friends from school? Why are you suddenly acting like your parents, who fall asleep on the couch as soon as dinner is over?

Well, as you've come to discover, work can be *exhausting*! It's a lot different than spending a few hours a day in classes or a few hours studying. The workday is all-consuming. The thought that you have to get up the following day and do it all over again can wipe you out.

When in college, you may have visited your family or even friends who were out on their own. Looming over your head was a huge sociology final. You thought about how nice it must be to be out of school, to not have to constantly worry about studying and writing papers. It would be nice to come home, prop your feet on the coffee table, and know that your day is done.

Now you know differently. Both worlds have completely different pressures and expectations. Both are exhausting in their own ways. Many different demands are placed on you now, and they can steal your strength. They rob you of your desire to do anything but relax after a hard day at work.

There's nothing wrong with you. A day at work—whether you stood in front of the copy machine all day, taught a classroom full of second-graders, or even split the atom—is exhausting. You will feel tired after work. So relax and get re-energized.

95.

Take Your Career
at Your Own Pace

Perhaps you are getting pressure from friends or family because they feel you are moving too slowly in your career. However, you are quite content with your entry-level position. You're happy with your responsibilities. You don't mind doing the mundane chores that your position often requires. In fact, you find something soothing about it. There's a security in knowing how to do something, and do it well. Why would you want to take a step up when you've finally mastered what's taken you a few months to achieve?

Don't let friends or family pressure you to feel otherwise. You need to manage your career at your own pace. Being content where you are is perfectly acceptable. There's nothing taboo about maintaining a nice, even keel.

Your friends and family may beg to differ. They might view the fact that you have been at your entry-level job for some time as demonstrating a lack of motivation. Don't let it get to you. In their way, your friends and family actually mean well. They want you to succeed. The problem is that they want you to succeed at *their* pace, not the one you've set for yourself.

And don't be afraid of the word "content." It's not something that middle-aged people feel once they've settled down with a house, a few kids, and a golden retriever. "Content" might be the exact opposite of what you wanted in college. Back then, you enjoyed the challenges, the frantic schedules, hectic pace, and late nights. Your friends may have even laughed at someone who was "content." But being content is good—if it feels good to you.

Move your career along at your own pace. You'll know when you're ready to take the next step.

96.

Reconnect with
Your Old Friends

Sometimes it helps to take a step back from your own life and consider what is going on in the lives of your friends and family. It's very easy to get swept away in your new world. Before you know it, all of your friends have drifted off. You can't even see them anymore—both figuratively and literally.

There was a time for letting your friends go and allowing yourself the chance to explore the world on your own. Now that you've got a handle on your little corner of the world, give your old friends a call, or drop them an e-mail and check in. In the back of your mind, you've probably heard a little voice saying, "I should call and see how so-and-so is doing." Don't keep pushing it off, telling yourself you'll get to it when you have a spare minute.

Spare minutes don't just drop into your lap. You have to put aside the time yourself and pick up the phone. After finally making the time, you might actually find that your friend is too busy to speak to you. Don't grumble about it after you hang up. Realize that reconnecting with your old friends is also like reconnecting with your old self. It helps you to refocus and remember why you even graduated college in the first place.

Most likely, when you call your old friends, they'll be happy to hear from you. A little voice has probably been nudging them in the backs of their minds, too. They'll be glad that you called.

97.

Recognize When
Your Values Have Changed

Things that you value are things that are important to you. Your values can often be your opinions and the way you view the world. In college, you were probably very aware of your values. You valued your time with your friends. You valued your freedom. You may have valued bucking the system, and speaking up for causes that no one else would speak for. These were the things that mattered to you. You saw the world in a certain way in college—and you never thought that you'd see it differently.

But you do now. It's hard to believe, and even harder to understand. How did this happen to you? Instead of working against the system, you're actually working within the system. You may still try to assert your college values on some level, but deep down, you might have realized that it's easier to go with the flow than to swim into the rip tide.

This is perfectly fine. You shouldn't feel like you've failed your old self. Part of being a college student is discovering the world on your own terms, questioning that world, and wondering how all of the problems arose. Even if the world were perfect, you wouldn't have seen it that way. You were a college student! It was your duty to point things out that the rest of the world was too dumb to realize.

The trouble is that you are no longer a college student. In fact, you haven't been for several months. And even more disturbing may be the day when you realize that you've actually become part of "the rest of the world." Without noticing it, the things that you once held near and dear—like changing the world and making a difference—have taken a backseat to merely surviving interviews, your job, paying bills, and other responsibilities.

Your life has changed, and most likely, so have your values. Your old values have been replaced. Accept that there is nothing wrong with either set of values. At some point, though, you will have to let one set go, because your life will not have room for both sets. And letting go of your old values will actually make you feel a lot freer.

98.

Maintain a Hobby to
Keep Your Groove

O ne of the reasons you might have feared or fought against the "real" world was because you were afraid that compromise meant giving up some of your identity. Perhaps if you've been at it and in it for a while, you might think that that's exactly what has happened.

Keep life in perspective. You've given up a lot. That's what growing up is all about. You realize that when you think back on all the things that you used to do in college. Now it seems that you don't do anything but work. You don't have time for anything else.

Try to make time for yourself. Reestablish who you were—and who you *are*. It's very easy to lose yourself when your career gets going and you try to meet the demands of the real world. The carefree, inspired you gets pushed aside by the responsible, hard-working you.

What was your "thing" in college? What did you really love to do? Try to do it now. Did you love skateboarding? Go to a skateboard park. Were you into photography? Pick up the camera again. Did you think you'd write the great American novel? Write a few paragraphs on your computer.

Like reconnecting with friends, you need to reconnect with yourself. Pick up an old hobby, and make it new again. In the process, you'll renew yourself, as well.

99.

Find an Activity That Relaxes You

Have the pressures and stress of everything you've gone through since college become too much? Your boss, your parents, and even some friends may tell you what to do. You are learning to manage your finances, take care of yourself, and maintain your own sense of self.

In order to keep your life and responsibilities in perspective, it helps to find one activity that can relax you. You need an outlet for the daily pressures of life. Choose an activity that really makes you feel good. Do you enjoy going to baseball games? Do you love curling up on the couch with a good book? Maybe you love hiking outdoors, or biking, or rowing on the river. Maybe what relaxes you is an evening out with your significant other.

We all need time out. Release that tension. Find an activity that relaxes you. It will have big results for your state of mind. Doing something that takes your mind away from your pressures will reenergize you for another day.

100.

Grab the Proverbial Bull
by the Horns

Life after graduation is exciting. It's also confusing. There's no easy way to make the transition from full-time student to full-time member of the "real" world. You can take it in steps, at your own pace, or even full steam ahead. It's still a huge transition, one fraught with headaches, stress, and self-doubt.

We are so confident in college. We feel like we can do anything! Then somewhere down the line, when dealing with home issues, job issues, or bad interviews, we lose that confidence. Now that we have been given our degrees, we are expected to stand on our own.

The most powerful tool you have at your disposal is not your college degree. It's not your family connections. It's not the great internship that you can put on your resume. The most powerful tool you have is *you* and your attitude toward facing your new life.

Try to keep inspired. Try to look at the world as something that needs to be conquered, something that you need to jump on with all the determination you can find and hang on for the wild ride ahead. The ride will be bumpy, filled with ups and downs, highs and lows. How will you handle yourself? Will you be able to hang on, or will you fall flat on your face?

Remember how you felt in college. Keep that energy with you. Don't let the everyday stresses of life drag you down. Grab the bull by the horns and hold on tight. Take charge of your life. If you can do so, your dreams will become very satisfying realities.